Mailships of the Channel Islands

SOUTHAMPTON HARBOUR 1838 (above) ST. HELIER HARBOUR 1840 (below)

MAILSHIPS

of the

CHANNEL ISLANDS

1771-1971

by

RICHARD MAYNE

First Published 1971 by Picton Publishing,

63 St. Mary Street, Chippenham, Wilts.

© Richard Mayne 1971

Printed by Picton Print.

I dedicate this book

To my long suffering wife Jean,
whose patience will be best understood
by any wife whose husband has a hobby.

COURIER, BUILT 1847 (below)　　　　　　　　HMS DASHER, BUILT 1837 (above)

Acknowledgements

I am greatly indebted to many people, institutions and museums for their invaluable assistance in the compilation of this work, especially my friend J.D. Attwood of Southampton who so often came to the help of a landlubber wallowing in the unfamiliar statistics of naval construction, hardly knowing the sharp end from the other. Raymond Falle of the Public Library, Jersey, J.A.C. West of the Weymouth Public Library, F.D.Y. Faulkener, ex P.R.O. British Transport Commission. Public Records Office, London. National Maritime Museum. Howard Robinson, Ohio, U.S.A. H. Gallichan, ex British Railways, Jersey. The following kindly supplied some of the rare photographs:-

Miss P.J. Ouless L.R.AM. A.A. Labbé. L.R. Tostevin. Jersey Evening Post Curator of the Dover Museum. Société Jersiaise Museum. British Rail.

DINARD (above)   DEVONIA (below)

Contents

THE SOUTHAMPTON MAILCOACH

The Eighteenth Century

Southampton had been from earliest times, the most favoured port connecting the Channel Islands with the mainland although no vessel had been used specifically for mail until 1794.

When anyone from the Islands wrote letters addressed overseas they handed them to merchants, or coffee house keepers, who were self-styled postmasters. The letters were then given to the Captain of the first available vessel sailing to England. On reaching Southampton the Captain handed over his bundle of letters to the receiving agent, who in turn placed them in the care of the official Postmaster, whereupon they commenced their sometimes arduous journey to the recipient.

These merchants, agents and Captains each charged a penny for their services and when the letter reached the addressee he or she had to pay the postage charges. This varying with the distance the letter had to travel.

It may seem strange to us today but prior to December 5th, 1839, it was the recipient who paid the postage on letters, and it can be imagined that the poorer friends and relations of islanders living, shall we say in Scotland, received their mail with mixed feelings, as in 1638 a letter from Jersey to Scotland cost one shilling and fivepence.

On the commencement of hostilities between Great Britain and France in 1778, the EXPRESS, an ex-Dover packet commanded by Captain Samson, was placed on the Southampton-C.I. run by orders of the Postmaster General, to carry mail and keep communications open. The EXPRESS was fully armed and cost the Post Office a considerable sum from which it derived little advantage as Captain Samson, delivered the letters as ship letters, receiving one penny each, the same as a master of any common vessel. On conclusion of peace in 1783 the EXPRESS returned to her station at Dover.

Various names of vessels, and their Captains, engaged in keeping open communications between the Islands and Southampton have been noted in the newspapers of the period. It may be worth while mentioning them here.

1780–1790's
JERSEY PACKET. Captain De St. Croix. 39 tons 4 crew
GUERNSEY PACKET. Captain Mourant. 39 tons 3 crew
SOUTHAMPTON PACKET. Captain Neel. 29 tons 4 crew
ALDERNEY PACKET. Captain Le Ray. 30 tons 3 crew

1

1785—1790's
POSTILLION PACKET. Captain Le Ray.
LIBERTY PACKET. Captains Simpson (later Wilkins and Durrel)
DISPATCH. Captain Babot.
PRUDENT. Captain De la Perrelle.   35 tons
CHARLOTTE. Captain P. Gallie.   18 tons 5 crew

1789—1790's
JOHANNA. Captain Bisson   40 tons 10 crew
SWIFT. (Brig) Captain Simon Dubois

1793—1809 at least
SPEEDY PACKET. Captain Henry Wilkins. 70 ton cutter, armed, carrying passengers, letters and parcels.
HERO. Captain Nicolle. Armed with 4 guns and carrying passengers
ROSE. Captain De Gruchy. Armed with 4 guns and carrying passengers
fare to Southampton, 21/-

An advertisement in the Gazette de L'isle December 31st, 1778, states 'Captains Thomas Payne and Jean Mauger, commanders of the cutter LA CHARLOTTE will take letters and parcels to St. Malo.' This vessel was of 18 tons and manned by 4 crew, but this venture soon faded out, for in 1792 we read, 'A proposition from agents and others to run a packet boat twice a week from Jersey to St. Malo. The boat will be paid for by subscription, anyone interested please write to this newspaper.' If anyone had interest they soon lost it, as war with France commenced the following year.

ST. HELIER HARBOUR 1780

Proof that a Post office of sorts, was in operation in Jersey is given in the notice which appeared in local newspaper of January 6th, 1787, 'Philip Hamon holding the post of letters in St. Helier informs the public that in future he will not admit anybody to enter his office during the time he is distributing the letters, as it was not the custom of any country, and, as he was owed a considerable amount of money, he begged his debtors to come and pay, otherwise he would refuse to deliver any more letters if they did not come and pay at once. Also he needed them to bring small change as he did not always have enough on him!

The service from these Post Offices was very lax. An incident is given in the 'Acts of the States' of 1789 where an account is given of a letter addressed to Stephen Cottril, of the Privy Council, from the States of Jersey apologising for the delay 'in answering your last letter, as it has been laying at the Post Office for over a fortnight.'

A Mr. Pierre Mallet was also a Postmaster at St. Helier for in the 'Gazette' of 1792 we read 'the brig LIBERTÉ, Captain Charles Hocquard, leaves Jersey on the 3rd June for St. Lawrence, Newfoundland. Those who have any letters for the north or south please contact Mr. Pierre Mallet who will look after them.' Those were the days when hundreds of Channel Islanders were engaged in the cod fishing industry around the Grand Banks off Newfoundland.

In November, 1793, the Gazette stated, 'the communications between the islands being long and uncertain, a boat will sail once a week to Lyme. Letters and packets for England may be left with Madame Anne Anley of Hill St. who will take the money, one sou for each letter or packet, addressed to Mr. Henry Chard, agent of Lyme. These boats will also call at Guernsey.'

War commenced with France in 1793 which put paid to the activities of small unarmed boats plying in the Channel which was a hotbed of enemy privateers on the lookout for plunder. In fact during the first two years of the war Jersey lost two thirds of her shipping, and 900 men were taken prisoner. These were disasterous times for the inhabitants and communications were very hazardous and uncertain.

In 1787 discussions were held between Christopher Saverland, a Post Office surveyor, and Mr. Palmer, the Controller General of the General Post Office in London, when Saverland proposed that vessels should be employed to sail from Portsmouth to Guernsey twice per week and the mail for Jersey should be carried by vessels which constantly run between the two islands. In fact Saverland hired 3 vessels for this service but nothing ever came of it.

Four years passed before the British Post Office instructed the Postmaster of Southampton to count the letters received from the Channel Islands for one month. This was done and amounted to 2,296 or 600 per week roughly 30,000 per year.

In Jersey, weary of continued requests for an official Post Office, merchants and businessmen decided to do something about it themselves. At a meeting of the Chamber of Commerce on the 11th May, 1790, it was resolved that a committee be held on the 22nd to consider the proposal of Edward Fiott Esq., with regard to the establishment of a Post Office in Jersey, and for Messrs. Fiott and P.H. Laurens to draw articles of regulations.

On the 21st May, Fiott and Laurens produced a sketch of regulations for a Post Office. Apparently this project was abandoned because no further discussion can be traced in subsequent Chamber of Commerce meetings.

Meanwhile in England much correspondence was going on between Saverland and the Secretary of the General Post Office, Francis Freeling and thence to the Postmaster General, on the subject of a postal service to the islands and weighing up the pros and cons of which English port would best suit the service. The government was also under the continued pressure from the Lieutenant-Governors of both Jersey and Guernsey.

On the 12th April, 1793, Henry Dundas, M.P., requested the Post Office to establish a 'packet service, similar to the method adopted in the last war, for the conveyance of packets and letters.'

A letter from Francis Freeling to the Postmasters General of the 1st February, 1794, reads:-

'My Lords,

By a letter I have this day received from Mr. Saverland at Weymouth, I understand that the ROYAL CHARLOTTE packet, Captain Wood, has arrived at that port. I have therefore given instructions to the Presidents of the Inland office to make up a mail for the Islands of Guernsey and Jersey on Wednesday next.'

The Post Office Cutters

The ROYAL CHARLOTTE under Captain James Wood sailed from Weymouth and arrived in Jersey with the first mail on the 18th February, 1794. The other vessel which joined the ROYAL CHARLOTTE was the ROVER, built at West Cowes in 1789, 67 tons and 53 feet in length, commanded by Captain Joshua Bennet. During the war they were armed with carriage guns and small arms. The third packet the EARL OF CHESTERFIELD, 78 tons and 56 feet in length, joined the service in June 1795 after being built at Bridport in Dorset.

The crossing from Weymouth (in good weather) took these cutters 16 hours for a distance of 85 miles.

The packets sailed to the Channel Islands for the first few months on a Thursday but on the 16th August, 1794, the States of Jersey wrote to the Earls of Chesterfield and Leicester, the Postmasters General asking for the date of sailing from Weymouth to be altered to any day but Thursday and to shorten the stay of the packet in Guernsey, owing to inconvenience.

Francis Freeling replied on the 7th October 1794, altering the sailing from Weymouth to Saturday but not shortening its stay in Guernsey. This correspondence was an official recognition by the States of Jersey of His Majesty's Post Office, as the Act of 1794 (34 George III XVIII 1794) had never been registered by the Royal Court of the Island, although it had in Guernsey.

Owing to the infrequent sailings of the Post Office packets various cutters and scouts as they were called, were loaned to carry the mail. Each governor of the Islands had a scout for his dispatches during the war, as did the Commander in Chief of the British Naval Squadron stationed at Jersey.

The names of some of these vessels were the MARY (armed scout) belonging to Sir John Doyle, Lieutenant-Governor of Guernsey, who also loaned his vessel for Post Office service after the CHESTERFIELD was captured in 1811. BRITTANIA Captain Naylor, BRILLIANT Captain Court, SIR SYDNEY SMITH, SIR WILLIAM CURTIS, Captain Batton and RAPID Captain White. The ROYAL CHARLOTTE was withdrawn from service about June 1795.

The EARL OF CHESTERFIELD was sold in Weymouth in 1806 but the son of Captain James Wood, Captain Starr Wood took command of a vessel named CHESTERFIELD and continued in the Post Office service. In the columns of the Gazette are incidents in the life of these cutters some exciting, some tragic. On the 4th March, 1809, we read:-

'As the gunner of the ROVER packet tried to get on board in St. Helier's harbour he fell and killed himself'.

Later on the 17th June, 1810, the CHESTERFIELD packet rescued a boat with five little boys on board which was drifting towards the rocks off Guernsey. An incident of a more serious nature took place on the 12th July, 1810, when a French privateer, cruising between Jersey and Guernsey attacked the CHESTERFIELD which had left Guernsey at 11.00 a.m. Captain Starr Wood says: 'At 6.00 p.m. South West of Portland West South West, two leagues. At 8.30 p.m. he ranged alongside within pistol shot. It was a large lugger and had 14 guns and was full of men. We gave him our broadside which made him sheer off'. The CHESTERFIELD was lucky, but one not so fortunate was His Majesty's hired cutter QUEEN CHARLOTTE commanded by Captain Thomas, twenty-five crew and eight guns, who, on the 29th August 1810, having on board Mr. P. Mulgrave charged with dispatches from the Commander in Chief of Jersey to the cruisers off Cherbourg, was attacked by a large French cutter off Alderney. It had 14 guns, 100 crew and flew the British flag, but on nearing the QUEEN CHARLOTTE, the Frenchman quickly changed colours, and hoisted the French flag. He then opened fire and the battle raged for one and a half hours until the Frenchman, experiencing such fearful fire, sheered off. The QUEEN CHARLOTTE's coxwain and two seamen were killed and twelve were wounded, Mr. Mulgrave received a shot in the head which deprived him of an eye. The injured crew were landed at Alderney to receive medical aid and the dead were buried in Jersey on Friday, 31st August.

On the 29th October, 1811, the CHESTERFIELD packet, on her way to Guernsey, was attacked and captured by a Cherbourg privateer the L'EPRUVIER, mounting 14 guns with a crew of 50. One passenger was killed, and several of the crew were injured, but the mails and dispatches were sunk prior to the boarding of the enemy. With the compensation of £1,626 paid to her owner by the Post Office Captain Starr Wood purchased another vessel and also named it CHESTERFIELD, built at Portland in 1812 of 107 tons and 63 feet in length.

The Treasury Letter Books of 1813–1814 contain an account of the unauthorised service of Captain Starr Wood of the CHESTERFIELD in 1813. He had been dismissed previously for 'the grossest misdemeanour' the details of this affair have not yet come to light, but I believe it was connected with a Mr. Rodber the Weymouth agent. Since his dismissal he had set up a packet in competition with the regular Post Office vessels, he even lured soldiers on board and carried an official box of money marked G.B. and had the presumption to imitate the Post Office packet flag. Passengers were led to believe that they were really on board one of His Majesty's packets.

Captain Starr Wood and the CHESTERFIELD are not mentioned after January, 1814, so it is presumed the authorities stopped his illegal deception.

To give an example of the frequency and severity of the actions of French privateers during the period from 1793 to 1814, 10,871 British vessels were captured.

An incident, fortunately more humourous that the last, was in January, 1814, when the Government scout BRILLIANT under the command of Captain Court, on a voyage from Guernsey to Southampton was captured by the American privateer PRINCE DE NEUFCHATEL, of 325 tons, twenty guns and 180 crew. A prize crew were put aboard BRILLIANT and she was headed for France but mistook Alderney harbour for the French port of La Hocque, entered the harbour and was promptly recaptured.

GENERAL DOYLE
In 1807 a third packet was added and the crossing was made twice per week. This third packet was the GENERAL DOYLE, commanded at first by Captain Ed Billot, then later by Captain Pipon. Two years later in the Gazette of 1809, we read: 'GENERAL DOYLE packet, built 1803, at Cowes in the Isle of Wight, a copper fastened cutter of 83 tons. The hull to be sold in consequence of a late Post Office regulation not allowing clinker built vessels to be employed in the service on account of the Smuggling Act. Apply Captain Pipon Weymouth, Francis Janvrin of Jersey, or Messrs Cary and Macullock of Guernsey'. Her last voyage as a mail packet was November 1809. This 44' cutter was bought by P. Poignard and Captain J. Le Masurier of Jersey and continued running privately between the Islands, in March of 1829, she was sold to W. Le Lacher of Guernsey.

Due to weather conditions and the activities of French privateers in the Channel, the sailings of these little packets were most irregular and on the 5th June 1809, the three packets arrived in St. Helier's harbour the same day.

ROVER was out of service by 1812.

HINCHINBROOK and FRANCIS FREELING
Two extra sailing packets were added to the Channel Island station in 1811, the HINCHINBROOK commanded by Captain Thomas Quirk and the FRANCIS FREELING by Captain Pipon. These vessels were built in 1811 for their owners who were the captains and were of 90 tons, with a fore reef mainsail, double reef foresail and a storm jib. The HINCHINBROOK and FRANCIS FREELING ran for 15 years, until Thursday evening the 2nd February, 1826, when the HINCHINBROOK under Captain Quirk, on a voyage from Weymouth to Guernsey struck the rocks near Longy, Alderney. So sudden was the shock, that the crew and passengers, twenty three in number, had scarcely time to save themselves, and the mail bags, before she went down. There was only one lady on board, and she was the only person to save her trunk, which floated from the stricken vessel, and was later picked up. It was reported that the crew had not conducted themselves as they should have done and an enquiry was held in the Guernsey Royal Court, where their conduct was judged blameless, however, Captain Quirk was held responsible for an error of judgement and pensioned off at the age of sixty seven.

On the night of the 6th September 1826, nearly seven months later, the FRANCIS

FREELING was run down by a Swedish brig off Portland, whilst on her way to Guernsey during a tempestuous gale, the darkness of the night and the violence of the storm, rendered rescue impossible, all the passengers, seven in number, and the crew of nine with the mails were lost. The wreckage was later washed up on the Dorsetshire coast. A liberal subscription was entered into at Weymouth and the Islands for the widows and orphans.

COUNTESS OF LIVERPOOL

The 22nd January, 1814, saw the maiden voyage to the Islands of the packet COUNTESS OF LIVERPOOL, under the command of Captain Robert White, who fortunately, at the time of her demise was not on board his previous vessel FRANCIS FREELING. His new vessel was of 104 tons, and had a crew of nine including the captain.

In 1819 the COUNTESS OF LIVERPOOL rescued the crew of the COURIER a sailing vessel from Rio, which was foundering off the Islands.

After 1826 when the HINCHINBROOK and FRANCIS FREELING were wrecked, the COUNTESS OF LIVERPOOL carried the mails alone between Weymouth and the Channel Islands for about a year until the advent of the first official steam packets in 1821. She was eventually bought by the Post Office from her owner Captain Robert White for £1,677 14s. 8d. and resold by them in 1827.

Up until 1818, the commanders of the packets each received £408 16s. 1d. per annum from the Post Office. This was indeed a paltry sum and to supplement their wages the crew actively engaged in smuggling, this activity actually leading to the abolition of all clinker built vessels in Post Office service in 1809.

In 1819 the Post Office granted the captains £238 16s. 1d. each per annum, plus all the fare money paid by passengers. The fare from Weymouth to Jersey in those days being 26/- for 'ladies and gentlemen and 13/- for servants', but even then these vessels were operating at a loss due to the advent of steam. Two private companies had been running the paddle steamers ARIADNE and the LORD BERESFORD from 1824 between Southampton and the Channel Islands, which of course were much quicker, more reliable and had better facilities for passengers, consequently causing the sailing packets, in the latter years to run almost empty.

Thus the year 1827 saw the end of these robust little vessels and their gallant crews, which had braved the elements, rocks and privateers for thirty three years.

In past accounts of this service, one frequently comes upon the mention of the steam yacht ROYAL CHARLOTTE. This vessel was in fact a sailing ship of 91 tons, built in 1821, Captain Godfrey commander, whose service was between Southampton and the Channel Islands, commencing in November 1821, she carried 40 passengers and had 16 to 20 beds. An advertisement in the local paper of the time stated that 'the greatest attention will be paid to the delivery of packages and letters, and sails once per week' this obviously in contravention of the Post Office Act. ROYAL CHARLOTTE was transferred to the Weymouth station in September 1823, and the following month she foundered in a gale off Cap De La Hague.

The Post Offices of Jersey and Guernsey

On the 13th February, 1794, the ROYAL CHARLOTTE packet arrived at St. Helier from Weymouth with Christopher Saverland, a post office surveyor, on board, who from the start had been instrumental in laying the foundations for postal services to operate to the Channel Islands. On arrival Saverland went immediately to the house in Hue Street with the warrant for Charles William Le Geyt and informed him of his appointment as Jersey's Post Master.

Le Geyt was born in the year 1733, son of Charles Le Geyt (Constable of St. Helier 1726–1733) and Martha de la Faye, and was from the same family as Phillipe Le Geyt, who was Lieutenant Bailiff from 1676–1710. Charles William Le Geyt joined the army in 1759, was commissioned and fought at the famous battle of Minden where he commanded a company of Grenadiers. In 1763, at the end of the seven years war, he was placed on half pay as a captain of the 63rd Regiment of Foot. He married Elizabeth Shebbeare in Soho, London, they later returned to Jersey and lived then at St. Saviour, later they moved to Hue Street. Le Geyt took an active part in Jersey politics, in fact in 1772 he took a monster petition to the Privy Council demanding a Royal Commission to investigate complaints from Jersey.

Le Geyt received his postal appointment with some surprise and the evening of the same day he wrote a letter to Evan Nepean, the then Under-Secretary of State for War, thanking him for his friendship and kindness, he (Le Geyt) having had no previous notice of his appointment.

A notice in the Gazette de L'isle of 1795 gives an idea of the hours that Le Geyt worked:-

'The post office is open every day from 9.00 a.m. until 3.00 p.m. and from 4.00 p.m. until 9.00 p.m. on the day the mail is to be made up. No letters will be given out from the hour mentioned until the mail is finished. The packet sails from Weymouth every evening.'

Eleven hours a day, seven days a week, apart from fetching the mails from the packet, making it up and passing it over to the recipients because in the early days the public had to call for their letters at the post office. In fact Le Geyt had to write out the names of people who had letters awaiting and these lists were placed outside four of the town hotels, which were 'The King's Arms' (Mr. Deal), 'The Union' (Mr. Aubin), 'The British'

(Mrs. Le Tublin)and 'Routs' (Mr. Rout). Le Geyt also felt obliged to entertain the captains of the packets to dinner, etc.

Later the same year Le Geyt had to accept the passage money of anyone travelling on the packet and to make out an order for the captain to receive them. If all this was not enough, people came knocking on his door after 9.00 p.m. to claim letters, which in exasperation caused Le Geyt to insert the following in the local paper:-

'Post Office, Jersey. In future, letters may be left without payment, it will suffice to drop them in the box. The Postmaster is willing for the convenience of the public, to put up a list in his office as soon as possible of letters that he has remaining in his care as well as the lists already outside the hotels. The public are asked to read these notices so as to spare the Postmaster answering questions when the office is closed. He will not give up letters until the office is open. Although he is aware that someone has complained of paying twopence for each letter after the hour of closing, he does this to save their grumblings, footsteps and purse, the alternative being to keep these letters for the next packet, or bring them in time, as they are unable to plead ignorance when the hour of closing is advertised in different parts of the town.'

During December, 1797, Le Geyt advertised 'for a person of good character, sobriety, honesty and integrity, to carry letters. They must also read French and English and calculate money.' We do not know how many replies Le Geyt received, but he did procure the service of a woman named Mary Godfray who lived in Sand Street and delivered all the letters in the town. She received no official pay but charged a halfpenny for every letter delivered and it is on record that she carried her letters in a cross handled basket.

It was not until 1830 that Mary Godfray received any official remuneration, but in that year she was granted the princely sum of six shillings per week, and five years later, in 1835, she had a rise of one and sixpence. Forty-five years after Mary had commenced her post office appointment the President of the Jersey Chamber of Commerce forwarded an appeal for her to the Postmaster General in London asking for her 'to be retired on pension being nearly worn out in the public's service.' Unfortunately her rank did not qualify her for a pension and the request was refused.

The inhabitants of St. Aubin and Gorey also employed a carrier to bring the mail from St. Helier to these places, and letters were called for at the self-styled post offices in these towns. An advert in the Gazette states:- 'good lodgings, apply post office at St. Aubin.'

The postage rates between the Channel Islands and Weymouth were established in 1794 at twopence per single letter, i.e. one sheet of paper folded and sealed, and the postage from Weymouth to London was fivepence, so a letter from Jersey cost sevenpence. In 1796 it rose to ninepence, 1801 to tenpence, 1805 to elevenpence and by 1812 to 1s. 1d. per single letter. Double letters, i.e. two sheets of paper, were charged double, and so forth, these charges being paid by the addressee.

During the first year of his office, Le Geyt charged an additional 1d. on each letter but under a storm of protest in Jersey this charge was dropped and in 1795 he was given an extra allowance from the General Post Office to make up his loss.

From 1794 to 1795 Le Geyt received £50 per annum salary plus the extra penny he charged on each letter. In 1814 his salary was raised to £140 per annum. In 1815 Le Geyt asked to be allowed to resign his office in favour of his son, George William Le Geyt, which he did the same year, being then aged 82. He died in 1827 at the ripe old age of 94.

THE GUERNSEY POST OFFICE

The Guernsey Post Office was established the same year as the Jersey Post Office in 1794 by Henry Dundas, M.P., naming A.C. Macdougall as the postmaster, but it was actually Mrs. Ann Watson who was appointed Guernsey's first Postmistress at her address in the High Street (now Tyler's shoe shop). Mrs. Watson was succeeded by her son Nicholas, in June, 1814. The post office was transferred in 1841 to Commercial Arcade under William Fell, postmaster, until four years later when it was transferred to 16 Fountain Street under Arthur Forrest (who later became Jersey's postmaster from 1855–1869). It was again transferred in 1848 to Commercial Arcade until May, 1883, when it finally came to its present site in Smith Street.

Apart from the internal running of the Guernsey Post Office, arrangements had to be made to include the other islands of Alderney, Sark and Herm, as they came under the Guernsey Bailiwick, a variety of local sailing vessels undertook this service. Although Jersey and Guernsey had Government Post Offices established in 1794, Alderney was without until 1843, and Sark without until 1857. An official post office was set up in Herm from 1925 to 1938, as a Guernsey sub-office, but owing to decreasing business closed. From 1938 to 1969, when the Guernsey Board again opened a sub-office on becoming independent of the G.P.O., the tenant of Herm issued his own carriage labels which were a great success with the many thousands who visited this beautiful island. The present tenant of Herm is once again the island's postmaster but now acts under the instructions of the Guernsey Post Office Board.

The Paddle Steamers

MEDINA

Before proceeding with the official mailships, it is of interest to note that the first steamer to be seen in both Guernsey and Jersey was the MEDINA, a 130 ton paddle steamer, built in 1823 costing £7,000. She was hired to bring a Colonel Fitzgerald and his family with their furniture to Guernsey.

MEDINA left Guernsey and arrived in Jersey on the 11th June, 1823, her arrival causing great excitement. Thousands flocked to the pier to see this novelty and the captain made quite a lot of money in showing eager sightseers over this smoke belching monster. MEDINA departed the next day, and records prove that she did not return again, being mainly employed on the Isle of Wight service.

ARIADNE

On the 29th August, 1821, there appeared in the columns of the 'Gazette de L'isle' a notice to the effect that:- 'A public meeting will be held at the British Hotel in St. Helier, of subscribers to a steam vessel. The subscription book is at Mr. Robert Collyers.' We do not know the exact outcome of this meeting but in 1824 the ARIADNE was built. A three masted paddle steamer built by William Evans of Rotherhithe, carvel built and copper bottomed, she was of 132 tons, 117 feet in length and had two engines developing 72 h.p. ARIADNE was commanded by John Bazin (a famous Guernsey captain), her first trip to Jersey being made on the 29th May, 1824. The shareholders who had the ARIADNE built were Philip Nicolle (junior) 2 shares, Philip Nicolle 1 share, John Benest 1 share, John Bazin the vessels commander, 1 share. The other 25 shares were owned by 25 Southampton merchants. By the Jersey Customs register we know that by 1836, ARIADNE was owned by the South of England Steam Packet Company, and after several owners was finally broken up in 1852.

LORD BERESFORD

Thirteen days after the arrival of the ARIADNE the LORD BERESFORD a wooden paddle steamer appeared. Built in 1824 by William Scott, at Bristol, she was of 155 tons and 100 feet in length, with two 35 h.p. engines from the Neath Abbey works. LORD BERESFORD had two masts and was schooner rigged, being named after Jersey's Lieutenant-Governor. She was owned by twenty-one shareholders, John Westwood, Robert Masterman (commander), Mathew Amiraux and eighteen Southampton businessmen. These shares were re-sold in 1826 to Robert Collyer who had held the subscription book at the public meeting in Jersey in 1821. Later the LORD BERESFORD was owned by the British & Foreign Steam Navigation Company, running for 19 years on the Southampton C.I. service, and in the summer months making trips to France. She was transferred to Bristol in 1843 and ran for twenty years from Swansea to Ilfracombe, being broken up in 1863.

These two vessels having proved their superiority to sail cutters, caused a lot of agitation to the authorities to provide a steam mail service, and on the 26th June, 1826, George W. Freeling assistant secretary to the General Post Office, and other officials came to Jersey, in the paddle steamer WATERSPRITE to make arrangements for steam vessels to operate the mail service, their crossing from Weymouth taking eight hours.

WATERSPRITE OFF ST. HELIER 1830

WATERSPRITE re-named WILDFIRE in 1837.
Consequently on, Saturday, 7th July, 1827, the WATERSPRITE, under the command of Captain Frederick White, a 162 ton wooden paddle steamer, arrived at St. Helier with the first official mail carried by a steam vessel. WATERSPRITE built in 1826, had cost £8,750 and had a crew of twelve, including the commander, she had a boiler pressure of eight pounds.

In June 1836, WATERSPRITE was lengthened 20 feet at Cowes and had new engines of 80 h.p. fitted, arriving back on her station on Christmas day, 1836.

IVANHOE
WATERSPRITE was followed a few days later by the IVANHOE, under the command of

14

Captain Robert White, later by Captain Comben. Built in 1820 by J. & C. Wood at Greenock, of 158 tons, and 60 h.p. engines she also had a boiler pressure of eight pounds. IVANHOE originally ran from Holyhead to Dublin, initiating the steam era with the TALBOT in 1820. For the technically minded, she cost £6,352 and had a crew of twelve. IVANHOE was engined by Maudsley with two 30 h.p. side lever engines with cylinders 32 inches in diameter, a 3 foot piston stroke driving two 12 foot 6 inch paddle wheels, she was 18 feet 6 inches in breadth, 11 feet in depth and drew 7 feet of water. In 1837 IVANHOE ceased running to the Channel Islands.

LOSS OF PACKET H.M.S. METEOR OFF PORTLAND BILL 1830

METEOR

On the 5th April, 1828, the third paddle steamer was added. This was the METEOR, commanded by Captain Connor. Built in 1821 by Evans of Rotherhithe, of 190 tons with 60 h.p. engines by Boulton and Watt, METEOR had originally served on the Lisbon and Irish stations, later serving on the Weymouth to C.I. route for nearly two years except when she was refitting at Holyhead for nearly six months. IVANHOE was at Liverpool for new boilers, so for thirty-one days WATERSPRITE did the C.I. mail run alone.

Whilst on her way from Guernsey to Weymouth, on the 23rd February, 1830, METEOR struck the Church Ope rocks near Portland at 8.00 p.m. and foundered. All aboard were rescued, but at low tide over one hundred people stormed aboard and looted the hapless vessel, METEOR became a total loss.

FLAMER RE-NAMED FEARLESS (H.M.S.) AT WEYMOUTH
NATIONAL MARITIME MUSEUM

FLAMER renamed H.M.S. FEARLESS in 1837.
The FLAMER replaced METEOR, her first voyage to Jersey was on the 29th April, 1831. Built in 1831 by Fletcher and Farnall of Limehouse at a cost of £7,190, of 160 tons with 60 h.p. engines and twelve crew under Captain F. White (later Captains Liveing, Comben and Symonds). FLAMER was greatly superior to the other vessels.

An example of conditions of travel on these early paddle steamers can be imagined by reading an account of a voyage given in the newspaper, the Jersey Argus, of Tuesday the 9th February, 1836 'Letter from a passenger on board H.M.S. packet FLAMER from Guernsey to Weymouth, to his father in Jersey:-

"When we left Guernsey the wind was favourable, but in about two hours a sudden calm came on which was speedily followed by a white squall, the forerunner of a tremendous gale. About 4 o'clock we shipped a heavy sea which knocked in the larboard paddle box and sent the ship's bulwarks on that side and one of the lifeboats adrift. The mate, Roberts, had his collar bone put out. I do not know what we should have done without Captain Symonds, who gave orders with great spirit. At eleven o'clock we shipped another heavy sea which filled the places forward, as well as the boat on the booms, in the bottom

16

of which they had to make a hole to let the water out, and we were left quite unprovided with lifeboats. The captain found he could not reach Weymouth and took us to the Isle of Wight. We were very near landing at Lymington but finally reached this place (Weymouth) at two o'clock this day (Wednesday). Had we been a few hours longer we would have been out of coals. Neither the mail or stage coaches have come in yet, as it has snowed more in the last two days than it has in the last six years.''

FLAMER was transferred to the Admiralty in 1837 and renamed H.M.S. FEARLESS. She was withdrawn from the Weymouth to C.I. mail service in 1839. H.M.S. FEARLESS became a survey vessel and even up to 1937 her hulk was believed to be in existence.

LADY DE SAUMAREZ
Meanwhile the two private shipping companies from Southampton had not been idle. In 1836 the British & Foreign Steam Navigation company had built the LADY DE SAUMAREZ of 350 tons, she made her first trip to Jersey on the 6th January, 1836, carrying passengers and cargo only at first.

ATALANTA
Not to be outdone, the rival company, the South of England Steam Navigation Company, placed on service, on the 24th August, 1826, the ATALANTA of 400 tons, also sailing from Southampton. The reader will find more about these two vessels later.

There was always great rivalry between the two companies and the Post Office packets, and in January, 1836, Captain Comben of the Post Office packet IVANHOE challenged Captain Goodridge of the LADY DE SAUMAREZ to a race from Jersey to Guernsey. The IVANHOE left 40 minutes before LADY DE SAUMAREZ, but was passed off Grosnez in Jersey. The LADY DE SAUMAREZ arrived at Guernsey 35 minutes ahead, owing to the fact that she had recently had new improved paddles fitted.

Owing to the financial losses of the packet stations (the Weymouth station alone, from 1832 to 1836, lost £1,700 per annum) the Government transferred the packet service to the Admiralty in January, 1837.

In February, 1837, IVANHOE was withdrawn from Channel Islands service and transferred to the river Thames, renamed BOXER and employed as a tug. She was condemned in 1846.

FLAMER was renamed H.M.S. FEARLESS in May, 1837.

WATERSPRITE was renamed H.M.S. WILDFIRE in 1837, her last mail trip from the Channel Islands was the 19th April, 1845. H.M.S. WILDFIRE ended her days as a tender to the Flagship of the Nore Division, being at that time the oldest ship on the active list in the Royal Navy, she was finally broken up in 1888 after 62 years service.

H.M.S. PLUTO
H.M.S. PLUTO, of 396 tons, was built for the Admiralty in 1831 at Woolwich. She was a

CAPTURE OF THE SLAVE SHIP ORION BY H.M.S. PLUTO 1859

ILLUSTRATED LONDON NEWS

wooden paddle steamer and carried two 24 pounder guns. H.M.S. PLUTO arrived in Jersey on the 17th September, 1837, under Captain Comben, and ran until the 8th February, 1838, being only a relief packet to replace H.M.S. FEARLESS (away for a refit). After her service in the C.I. mail run, her activities included the capture of an American slave ship in 1850 off the west coast of Africa, a punitive expedition up an African river in January 1858, and capturing the slave ship ORION in 1859. H.M.S. PLUTO is out of records by 1863.

H.M.S. DASHER

On Sunday the 15th April, 1838, H.M.S. DASHER arrived on service. A 250 ton paddle steamer commanded at first by Lieutenant William Roberts, H.M.S. DASHER was built at Chatham especially for the Channel Islands mail run, she had two 50 h.p. engines, and a boiler-pressure of only eight pounds. This vessel carried mail between Weymouth and the Islands for seven years, whereupon under Commander W.L. Sheringham she was engaged in a survey of the south coast of England, this taking two years. In 1853, H.M.S. DASHER rescued the DISPATCH for which her then commander Lefebvre was promoted to Captain, in 1854 she went on service to the Crimea, and in 1856 to the naval review at Spithead. In 1860 our old friend was again stationed in the C.I. at Gorey harbour in Jersey but her work was now fishery protection, one of her commanders was Charles Anson who later became an admiral, he died in 1940. H.M.S. DASHER was replaced by H.M.S. MISTLETOE in 1884, and was finally sold in 1885.

H.M.S. CUCKOO SINKING IN ST. HELIER HARBOUR, MAY, 1850

ILLUSTRATED LONDON NEWS

H.M.S. CUCKOO

The next vessel placed on the mail run was H.M.S. CUCKOO, which had formerly been named CINDERELLA. Built in London in 1824 for owners operating the Irish mail run, H.M.S. CUCKOO was of 234 tons, with 100 h.p. engines, and carried the Island mails from 1839 until April 26th, 1845, when she was also transferred to Fishery Protection at Gorey, Jersey, replacing H.M.S. KITE. Whilst ferrying troops (bringing the 26th Regiment Cameronians and taking away the Dorsetshires) to the troopship H.M.S. BIRKENHEAD, anchored off Jersey, on May 14th, 1850, H.M.S. CUCKOO struck the oyster rock near Elizabeth Castle and just made it to the harbour mouth whereupon she sank, without loss of life fortunately, and was later refloated and returned to her station at Gorey until withdrawn in 1851 being replaced by H.M.S. DASHER. After service in the Baltic H.M.S. CUCKOO is out of records by 1864. One of her commanders was Jerseyman Henry Dumaresq who became an Admiral in 1875.

The railway reached Southampton by 1840 and, as the journey to London could be accomplished in three hours, gave an impetus to Southampton as a mail connection with the Channel Islands. Under pressure from various bodies in the islands, the post office allowed mail to travel via Southampton, but only if the writer endorsed in the right hand corner of the letter the words 'To Southampton by Private steamer', thus saving two days compared with the Weymouth packet service. In 1845, due to the hopeless competition, the mail contract was transferred from the Admiralty to the 'South Western Steam Packet Company' running from Southampton.

It may not be amiss here to quote passages from the life of one of the most famous captains of those early days, taken from Crabbs 'Life of Captain Bazin.'

CAPTAIN JOHN BAZIN OF THE 'ARIADNE'

'John Bazin was born the 7th March, 1780, at St. Peter Port, Guernsey, and was the eldest of fourteen children. His father was master and owner of the sailing ship THREE FRIENDS, young John was taken from school at the age of nine, and sent to sea, he was taken prisoner by a French frigate mounting 44 guns in 1793, when he was thirteen, off Cap de La Hague, six months later he was exchanged among others with French prisoners at Cherbourg, and landed back in Guernsey on the 2nd January, 1794. Bazin went back to sea again in his father's vessel, the BETSY trading chiefly to Alderney, in 1795 they made 68 voyages.

John Bazin's first command was in the BETSY, in 1796 when he was aged sixteen, his father allowed him 2s. 6d. per week pocket money. In 1798 his father bought the sailing vessel AGENORIA of 55 tons, and John Bazin assumed command at an increased wage of 5 shillings per week, later, he left the AGENORIA in the wish to educate himself, using his savings of twenty guineas, his father refusing to pay for his board or schooling. Later he returned to sea as master of his father's ship HARRY, in 1802 he married Mary Hall who lived in Jersey, she was eighteen. Whilst piloting H.M. Brig LIBERTY to Alderney, Bazin captured a large French brig bearing American colours, for which he later received £78 prize money.

After the HARRY Bazin took command of a new vessel the ACTIVE built at Southampton of 72 tons. With his family increasing he bought a shop in Fountain street, Guernsey, probably with his prize money, but he also continued his life at sea. At about the same time in 1805, his father died, leaving some property and money, little of which was left to his son John. In 1806 Bazin bought the ACTIVE cutter, and resold her for Government service. Under the orders of Sir John Doyle, the Lieutenant-Governor of Guernsey, Bazin assumed command until ACTIVE was lost on rocks off Castle Cornet Guernsey, fortunately he was ashore at the time. The vessel which replaced the ACTIVE was the scout SPEEDY a vessel he commanded employed mainly to carry Government expresses from Guernsey to England, with occasionally naval and military officers, SPEEDY carried a crew of 20, and mounted eight guns.

John Bazin was dismissed from Government service in September, 1814, but was given a handsome testimonial from Lieutenant-General Doyle, so obviously the circumstances of his dismissal could not have been very serious, and may have stemmed from his religious zeal, for he was a profound methodist, given to lecturing anyone who crossed his path.

His wife died, and in October, 1814, he moved to Jersey with his new wife and family, and took command of the SPEEDY PACKET trading between Jersey and Southampton, one of three vessels in the same trade, he also opened a shop in St. Helier, which his wife probably managed. In 1824 John Bazin supervised the building of the paddle steamer ARIADNE, and on June 6th of the same year she made her first passage to Guernsey under his command, he was by then living back in Southampton. ARIADNE was laid up during the winter from October to April. From 1827 ARIADNE called once per month at St. Malo, and from 1832 once per month at Granville. Because of the deteriation of his wife's health, the family left Jersey for Guernsey in 1833. During the winter of 1836, Bazin was employed by the South of England Steam Navigation Company to superintend the building of their newest steam paddleship, the ATALANTA in the Isle of Wight. John Bazin's son-in-law, Captain Babot (another great name in the Islands seafaring history) was appointed commander of ATALANTA.

John Bazin died on the 12th February, 1836, and was buried in St. Mary's churchyard in Southampton. Bazin was not popular with everybody, as he literally thrust religion down the throats of both his crew and passengers to an unbearable extent, even holding prayer meetings on board his vessel at every port, forcing his crew to attend. He forbade the playing of cards (which was a popular pastime to while away the hours of an uncomfortable voyage) on his ship, which caused the company's competitors to mention this in their advertisements. However he was a great man, and the quality of his seamanship was never in question.

The South Western Steam Packet Company

In 1842 the London & South Western Railway Company mainly financed the South Western Steam Packet Company, because at the time railway companies could not legally own ships, it was also L.S.W.R. money that paid for the acquisition of the Commercial Steam Packet Company, which had been formed some years previously. This South Western Steam Packet Company five years later absorbed the South of England Steam Packet Company and then changed its name to the New South Western Steam Navigation Company.

To complicate matters even further, journalists and others continued to refer to it as the South Western Company, which has been the cause of much confusion in previous endeavours to sort out which companies owned which ships.

Finally the London & South Western Railway Company took over completely (when the law had been changed) the New South Western Steam Navigation Company in 1862 and kept the name of London & South Western Company until 1932.

PADDLE STEAMER SOUTH WESTERN

SOUTH WESTERN

The first vessel to bring the official Southampton mail on the 27th April, 1845, was the SOUTH WESTERN under the command of Captain James Goodridge (father of two famous mailboat captains) who when master of the sail cutter CRACKER during the Napoleonic war, was captured and imprisoned by the French. The SOUTH WESTERN was built in 1843 by Ditchburn & Mare of Blackwall, she was an iron paddle steamer, the first to be placed on the Channel Islands run, of 204 tons, 143 feet in length and 18 foot beam. SOUTH WESTERN had first called at Jersey in 1843. In 1848 she ran from Poole to the C.I. with mail and cargo, and was eventually sold to a Japanese firm, who removed her paddle wheels, rigged her as a sailing vessel and sailed her to Japan.

TRANSIT

The TRANSIT, a wooden paddle steamer followed on the 28th April 1845, she was built at Poplar in 1835 for the British & Foreign Steamship Company, and first ran from London to Gibraltar. TRANSIT was 201 tons, 126 feet in length and her engines developed 80 h.p., she had first come to Jersey in August, 1839. TRANSIT was withdrawn from service to the Channel Islands in 1855, and ended her life as a coal hulk in Southampton docks in the 1860's.

WONDER

Next, on the 5th May, 1845, came the WONDER from Southampton and Guernsey, built like the SOUTH WESTERN the previous year for the South Western Steam Navigation Company at Blackwall by Ditchburn & Mare. WONDER was a 250 ton iron paddle steamer, 158 feet in length, 20 foot beam and 10 foot in depth, her paddle wheels were 19 feet in diameter. WONDER was one of the fastest steamers of her day, attaining the then high speed of 14 knots, in September 1844, WONDER beat in a race THE FAIRY (Queen Victoria's yacht), BLACK EAGLE, ECLIPSE, PRINCE OF WALES, METEOR, ISLE OF THANET, SAPPHIRE, BLACKWALL and RAILWAYS.

WONDER is also famous because of the terrible ordeal her passengers and crew underwent during a violent storm in October, 1846, the following extract is taken from the 'Guernsey Star' newspaper:- "When the WONDER left Southampton at 7.00 p.m., the weather was fair and with no apparent likelihood of the terrible storm, which commenced at 11 o'clock at night, and continued with scarcely any intermission until her arrival at St. Helier at 4.30 p.m. the following day, where her fearless and consumately skillfull commander (Captain James Goodridge Junior), was welcomed with three cheers by the crowd assembled on the piers......... Captain Goodridge stated that in all the countless passages he has made across the channel he never before experienced so boisterous a transit. When off the Casquets rocks she was, we understand, struck by a tremendous sea which carried away part of her bulwarks, and did various other damage and at one time she was completely thrown upon her side and many of her passengers were dashed from their berths to the floor of the cabin.........they were all shut down from the decks, as were also the crew, except those whose services were indispensable at the wheel, etc., whilst Captain Good-ridge himself dauntlessly kept his station between the paddle boxes. By his presence of mind alone, and his seamanlike management of his vessel, she was brought safely to

THE PADDLE STEAMER WONDER DURING THE STORM OF OCTOBER 1846

Guernsey..........where many of the Jersey passengers deemed it prudent to land. Captain Goodridge, however, decided to proceed to St. Helier where he arrived safely at 4.30.......... .....If ever a seaman deserved a public testimony of public admiration, the commander of the WONDER is that man and the testimony, we trust, will ere long be given to him.'' After a public subscription, Captain Goodridge was presented with a silver speaking trumpet and a piece of plate, and his first and second officers together with the chief engineer were given medals. An oil painting (Societe Jersiaise Museum) and lithographs depicting WONDER during this terrible storm are known.

WONDER was re-boilered in 1865, and in 1868 was placed on the Jersey to St. Malo mail route, the last reference to WONDER in local newspapers was in February, 1874. She was broken up in 1875.

There was a Southampton inn named after the WONDER near Northam Bridge from 1856 until demolished in 1958, the four coloured leaded lights depicting WONDER which were in the main door and side windows have been preserved.

CALPE
Following the WONDER on the 14th May, 1845, came the CALPE of 131 tons, a wooden

24

paddle steamer built in 1835 at Rotherhithe with engines of 89 h.p. She was owned by the Commercial Steam Packet Company and ran from London to Gibraltar, later she was transferred to the South Western Steam Packet Company, which in turn became the New South Western Steam Navigation Company, her first voyage with mail to these islands was, as stated 1845, but previously she had run here commercially. CALPE's two known commanders were Captains Lewis and Clements.

LADY DE SAUMAREZ
The following year, on the 15th May, 1846, we see the return of an old friend, the LADY DE SAUMAREZ, named after a famous Guernsey lady. This vessel was built by Henry Wimshurst of Millwall for the British & Foreign Steam Navigation Company in 1835—6, she was of 350 tons, 127 feet in length with a 20 foot beam and 80 h.p. side lever engines, the paddle wheels were fitted with Sewards Feathering floats. Forty two beds were provided for passengers in cabins fore and aft. LADY DE SAUMAREZ had made her first voyage to Jersey in January, 1836, with passengers and goods, then from 1840 she was allowed to carry endorsed mail, until the 15th May, 1846, she brought her first official mail, then being owned by the South Western Steam Packet Company. LADY DE SAUMAREZ was broken up in 1853.

PADDLE STEAMER 'ATALANTA' 1836—1869

ATALANTA
In opposition to the LADY DE SAUMAREZ the then rival company had built a beautiful two-masted, clipper bowed paddle steamer, the ATALANTA built by Thomas White at Cowes in 1836, she was of 400 tons, 140 feet in length and had a beam of 23 foot, ATALANTA was later lengthened another 20 foot. She had sleeping berths for 150 passengers, and her

building was supervised by Captain Bazin of the ARIADNE. Contemporary newspapers reported that "ATALANTA had a pair of side lever engines of 60 h.p. each, cylinders of 43 inches diameter with a 3 foot 6 inch stroke driving 16 foot 6 inch paddle wheels, steam being supplied by a flue boiler at 7 pounds per square inch. A splendid steam vessel, a more complete one of her description in every respect, we would say never kissed the salt water."

ON RIGHT, REMAINS OF ATALANTA IN ST. HELIER HARBOUR   1870

Like the LADY DE SAUMAREZ, ATALANTA's first official voyage with mail to the Channel Islands, was in April 1847, under the command of Captain Babot. ATALANTA ended her days as a coal hulk in St. Helier's Harbour during the 1890's.

MONARCH
A newcomer to the service on June 7th, 1847, was the MONARCH under the command of Captain Lewis. Built of wood by Rubie and Baker of Northam in 1836, a paddle steamer of 360 gross tons, 140 feet in length, with a 23 foot beam, her paddles were driven by engines developing 120 h.p. MONARCH was built in four months, and engined by Horseley & Company of Tipton for the South of England Steam Packet Company, later she was owned by the British & Foreign Steamship Company. MONARCH only carried the C.I. mail from June until November she was changed to cargo carrying only. In 1848 she towed the famous chinese junk KEYING to London. Eventually MONARCH was converted to a barque and sailed to New Zealand in 1849.

The Changes of Ownership

In 1847 the New South Western Steam Navigation Company was formed. It bought out the South Western Steam Packet Company's ships and property for £56,623, also the South of England Steam Packet's ships and property for £29,000, and in part cost of three new ships, EXPRESS, DISPATCH and COURIER, £42,870. This company was loaned £50,000, by the London & South Western Railway Company.

The new company re-newed the five year mail contract for £4,000 in April, 1848. The year 1851, saw the London Brighton & South Coast Railway Company sued by the South Eastern Railway Company for owning ships contrary to law, so afterwards the London Brighton & South Coast Company chartered vessels from a Mr. Maples a shipbroker, who had a cargo service from Littlehampton to the Channel Islands and from Newhaven to Dieppe. These ships were chartered for eleven years until the Act of Parliament of 1862, allowing the railway companies to own and operate ships.

Upon arrival in St. Helier's roads during the nineteenth century at low tide, passengers of paddle steamers had to be taken ashore by horse and cart, or if there was too much mud, carried on men's backs. This caused some irate correspondence in the Jersey newspapers of the period, and even caused Albert, the Prince Consort, to ask on his visit to Jersey, 'Why do you Jerseymen build your harbours on dry land?'

COURIER
A new iron paddle steamer was built by Ditchburn & Mare of Blackwall, in 1847, for the South Western Steam Packet Company, and especially for the C.I. traffic. COURIER was of 314 tons and engined by Maudsley. In fact Henry Maudsley accompanied her on her maiden voyage to the islands on the 12th November, 1847. COURIER had two funnels and a clipper bow and was commanded by Captain James Goodridge, who was previously in command of the MONARCH.

COURIER was withdrawn from service in 1875.

DISPATCH
The sister ship to the COURIER was the DISPATCH who made her maiden voyage to Jersey on the 2nd May, 1848. Owing to the low tide in August, 1848, her passengers had to be carried ashore on men's backs. DISPATCH was an iron paddle steamer with two funnels and a clipper bow. Her first trip was from Poole, which was then a newly made packet station. DISPATCH continued from Jersey to St. Malo and then returned to Poole, but was

later transferred to the Southampton station. She was commanded by the well-known Captain George Babot. DISPATCH was withdrawn from service in 1888.

DISPATCH PASSING CORBIERE, JERSEY

'DISPATCH' IN DISTRESS OFF LA MOIE SIGNAL STATION
17th OCTOBER, 1853

EXPRESS

The third of these vessels which were almost identical, was the EXPRESS, built at the same time and by the same builders as COURIER and DISPATCH. EXPRESS was 160 feet in length with a 22 foot beam and 11 feet in depth, her engines had annular cylinders 50½ inches in diameter with a 3 foot piston stroke which drove her 18 foot diameter paddle wheels at twenty eight strokes per minute, steam was provided by two tubular boilers with a pressure of 15 pounds per square inch.

THE EXPRESS 1847–1859

THE WRECK OF THE EXPRESS AT ST. BRELADE IN 1859

Before being placed on the Channel Islands station EXPRESS was given the important task of bringing Louis Philippe to Newhaven when he fled from France in 1848. She came to Jersey on the 28th May, 1848, and two years later had a refit costing £2,000. On a voyage from Jersey to Guernsey on the 20th September, 1859, the EXPRESS struck a treacherous group of rocks off Corbiere known as Les Boiteaux. She tore a hole in her port bow and made water fast, being eventually wrecked at St. Brelade. Two passengers panicked, jumped overboard and were drowned but the rest totalling one hundred and eight were saved including the crew. On board were three racehorses due to race in Guernsey the following day, and these were also rescued by mattresses and bed linen being placed on the slippery rocks enabling the terrified animals to reach terra firma. The regular commander of the EXPRESS Captain Harvey was absent being on another vessel and the first mate R.C. Mabb was in command. The illustration of the sinking of the EXPRESS is from a lithograph by P.G. Dutton after a painting by the Jersey artist P.J. Ouless.

ST. HELIER HARBOUR 1855

The Weymouth and Channel Islands Steam Packet Company

In 1857 a new company commenced running from Weymouth to the Channel Islands and France, this was the Weymouth & Channel Islands Steam Packet Company (mainly financed by the Great Western Railway Company) who commenced with two vessels CYGNUS and AQUILA. These two vessels were at first chartered from Mr. Maples the shipbroker, but eventually purchased by the W. & C.I.S.P. Company in November, 1857.

PADDLE STEAMER CYGNUS

CYGNUS

The CYGNUS an iron paddle steamer of 245 tons, was built in 1854 by Henderson & Sons of Renfrew, for the North of Europe Steam Navigation Company who ran the Harwich-Antwerp service which proved unsuccessful. CYGNUS had a length of 182 feet and a breadth of 20 feet, with two funnels and a clipper bow. Her maiden voyage to Jersey was the 11th April, 1857, CYGNUS earned £10,000, in salvage for the W. & C.I.S.P. Company when she rescued and took in tow a newly built vessel called the JOHN DIXON, loaded with cargo, being disabled off West Bay whilst on her maiden voyage.

CYGNUS was sold to an Isle of Man company in 1889, and resold to David MacBrayne & Company, for the West Highlands service in 1891. CYGNUS was re-named BRIGADIER, and her two funnels were replaced by one, a new figurehead was fitted and she was transferred to the Hebridean route. BRIGADIER (ex CYGNUS) was lost off the Isle of Harris in 1894.

PADDLE STEAMER 'AQUILA'

AQUILA

The sister ship, and almost identical in appearance as the CYGNUS, AQUILA followed six days later to the Channel Islands, having been built by the same builders, for the same company and to run on the same service as CYGNUS. AQUILA was commanded by Captain Philip Falle, and apart from her normal mail service also called at the other islands and France. AQUILA had a speed of 14 knots. In 1889 she was sold to the Plymouth, Channel Islands and Brittany Steamship Company of Guernsey, and continued her service to the C.I. and France carrying cargo and passengers only, and doing excursions in the summer. In 1896 AQUILA was sold to a company in Swansea and used for excursions to Llandudno, she was then known as ALEXANDRA, the following year she was owned by the Hastings St. Leonard's & Eastbourne Steamship Company and known as RUBY. AQUILA led a comparatively uneventful life and her only claim to fame was when she was chartered in 1870, to bring the fugitive Princess Eugenie from Ostend to England.

BRIGHTON

The third of this company's vessels was the BRIGHTON which was placed on C.I. service

PADDLE STEAMER 'BRIGHTON'

in May, 1857. BRIGHTON, an iron paddleship, had been built in 1856 for the London Brighton & South Coast Railway Company, by Palmer of Jarrow. Chartered at first by Maples & Morris, (shipbrokers) BRIGHTON was purchased in 1858 by the W. & C.I.S.P. Company, she was of 286 tons, 193 feet in length, and a beam of 20 foot, her paddles were driven by engines developing 140 h.p. making her one of the fastest ships of her day, she had a turtle back deck over the forecastle and five bulkheads. Her known commanders were Captains Knight, Painter and Brache. BRIGHTON ran on the Channel Islands station for thirty years until a voyage from Weymouth to Guernsey, on the 29th January, 1887, she struck the Brays rocks in the Little Russel and became a total wreck, sinking in fifteen minutes. Fortunately the passengers and crew were saved but the mails were lost. At a subsequent enquiry her captain was suspended for six months. A macabre detail from this event was that a coffin containing a body for Guernsey burial was washed up intact in Alderney.

The New South Western
Steam Navigation Company

PADDLE STEAMER 'ALLIANCE'

ALLIANCE

The next of the N.S.W.S.N. Company's vessels was the ALLIANCE. Built in 1855 by Mare of Blackwall, at a cost of £19,460, and named after the Anglo-French Crimean alliance. She was an iron paddle steamer of 311 tons, 175 feet in length and a beam of 23 feet, with Seward & Capel engines, 21 foot paddle wheels and a boiler pressure of 16 pound per square inch. The first voyage to Jersey was made on May 8th, 1860, she had new engines fitted in 1878 and new boilers ten years after, also one of her two funnels was removed. Her first years were spent mainly on the Southampton to C.I. mail run, but the rest of her time was employed between Jersey — St. Malo and Granville carrying passengers, mail and cargo with the occasional summer cruise. Captain F. Allix was her commander for a number of years.

ALLIANCE was sold and broken up in March, 1900.

PADDLE STEAMER SOUTHAMPTON

SOUTHAMPTON
The last vessel built for the New South Western Steam Navigation Company was the SOUTHAMPTON. Built in 1860 by Palmer of Jarrow, she was the largest ship then on C.I. service, and the strongest ship yet built in Britain, she was of 460 tons (hold measure) 232 feet in length, with a 22 foot beam, SOUTHAMPTON had two funnels, two schooner rigged masts, and a round stern, her paddle boxes were cased in with radiated gratings on which were painted the words 'Royal Mail Steamer' and a large crown underneath, her engines worked to a pressure of 16 pounds to the square inch. Her first voyage to Jersey was on the 13th October, 1860, and she was commanded by Captain James Goodridge and the crew of the old COURIER. SOUTHAMPTON had three re-fits which altered her appearance considerably. She was lengthened in 1875 and had one funnel removed in 1880. She was taken off C.I. service in 1897 and later used as a floating hostel for strikers in Southampton. This splendid vessel was sold to Dutch shipbreakers and broken up in March, 1898.

The London and South Western Railway Company

In 1862 an Act of Parliament was passed authorising the London & South Western Railway Company to own and operate ships. Consequently the L.S.W.R. Company took complete control of the New South Western Steam Navigation Company, which it had backed financially for years. Thus commenced a new era in Channel Islands mailship history.

The early records of the L.S.W.R. Company's vessels are a little difficult to place chronologically, because very few ships were on a permanent station. In the summer the service was supplemented by extra vessels and one ship might arrive in Jersey, take the passengers and mail to Southampton via Guernsey and perhaps the same ship would not return for months, having been placed on another station.

PADDLE STEAMER 'NORMANDY'

NORMANDY

The first vessel built for the London & South Western Railway Company's Channel Island service was the ill fated NORMANDY built in 1863 by J. Ash of London. Engined by J. Steward of Blackwall, she was an iron paddle steamer of 600 tons, 210 feet in length, a 24 foot beam with a speed of 15½ knots, NORMANDY had 130 passengers berths and carried 200 tons of cargo, her maiden voyage to Jersey being on the 19th September, 1863, commanded by Captain Babot, she was the first steamer on C.I. service to have a straight stem.

On a voyage from Southampton to the Channel Islands on the 17th March, 1870, during a storm NORMANDY was involved in a collision with a Baltic trader, the 1,400 ton S.S. MARY on her way from Odessa to London with a cargo of Indian corn, she rose above the NORMANDY and fell right across her mailboats deck crushing her superstructure causing the NORMANDY to sink in twenty minutes, with a loss of thirty-three lives including Captain Harvey and fifteen crew. Thirty-one persons were saved. The MARY was towed to Southampton, and the survivors were brought to Jersey by the HAVRE. The mails were lost, but later a floating bag was picked up and the mail delivered. A monument to this tragedy was erected in 1871 and is now to be seen on the junction of Jersey's Victoria pier and Mount Bingham.

PADDLESHIPS AT WEYMOUTH HARBOUR 1860

The Jersey-France Mail Service

From earliest times communications had been maintained between the Islands and various ports on the adjacent coast of France, chiefly St. Malo, Granville and Carteret, by cutters and various sailing vessels, of which there were many plying from Jersey and Guernsey. The first steamer to enter St. Malo was the paddle steamer ARIADNE in 1824 from Jersey.

The next year the LORD BERESFORD also joined the service from Jersey to St. Malo, and these two steamers continued to operate with the inclusion of Granville as a further port, from 1832 until 1833 when the GEORGE CANNING paddle steamer also joined this route. She was owned by six Jersey merchants, having been originally built as a sloop at Dumbarton in 1824, in 1831 she was re-built as a schooner 99 feet in length, and later refitted as a paddle steamer eventually being sold to a foreign firm. It is unlikely the GEORGE CANNING carried mail.

The CAMILLA paddle steamer of 132 tons, built at Rotherhithe for King & Company in 1834, for the Southampton to Havre run also did the Jersey to St. Malo route from 1837 to 1842, and was transferred to the Plymouth to C.I. service in 1843.

The GRAND TURK a 500 ton paddle steamer with 300 h.p. engines was built for the British & Foreign Steam Ship Company in 1837, her first voyage to Jersey was in 1838 under Captain Knight, part of her service was from Guernsey to Morlaix, once weekly. It is believed the GRAND TURK was bought by the L.S.W.R. Company in 1851, she ended her days as a coal hulk in Southampton.

The PRINCESS ROYAL a 100 ton steamer owned by the Jersey Steam Packet Company operated the C.I. to France route from June, 1845, until sold to a company in Alderney in 1847 for £1,200.

In 1847 the N.S.W.S.N. Company took over the service with the paddle steamer SOUTH WESTERN but for three years only.

QUEEN OF THE ISLES an 81 ton paddle steamer, built in 1853 carried mail between Guernsey, Alderney and Cherbourg from November, 1853, to July, 1872, under Captain G. Scott.

From 1850 to 1863 the mail service to St. Malo and Granville was operated by paddle steamers of the Jersey Steam Packet Company whose chief shareholder was Mr. F.C.

Clarke, the Jersey ship builder who indeed built the ROSE the second steamer to be built in Jersey. Of 83 tons, the ROSE was a wooden paddle steamer built at West Park and fitted with the boilers of the SUPERB, which was wrecked on the Minquiers rocks in 1850, a year earlier.

The other vessels of this company were the VENUS, COMETE, DUMFRIES and EDIN-BURGH CASTLE, all paddle steamers. COMETE and DUMFRIES were retained by the L.S.W.R. Company who bought out the Jersey Steam Packet Company in 1863, COMETE was re-named GRANVILLE and is out of records by the early 1870's.

The GUERNSEY was built in 1874 by J. & W. Dudgeon of Blackwall a 572 ton screw steamer with a speed of 13 knots, she was owned by the L.S.W.R. Company, and definitely carried mail in 1881. GUERNSEY was later converted to cargo, and eventually wrecked off Cap De La Hague with a loss of seven crew on the 9th April, 1915, there being no light from the lighthouse because of the war.

The other vessels of the L.S.W.R. Company, running to St. Malo and Granville, were: the GRIFFIN, the first screw steamer engaged in this service, originally built in 1858 and purchased by the L.S.W.R. Company in 1865 and was in service until about 1889.

The WONDER (ibid) was running to France from 1868 until 1870, when the old Southampton mailboat, DISPATCH (ibid) maintained the service until 1888.

THE CONTENTIN' AT GOREY, JERSEY

From 1888 up to 1896 a variety of London & South Western Railway Company's steamers operated this route including (ibid) CAESAREA, HONFLEUR, ALLIANCE, ST. MALO and FANNIE.

At the inauguration of Carteret harbour in 1881, a French company opened the Jersey to Carteret service, with the steamer CLAIRE, which ran until succeeded by the CONTENTIN of the same company, these two steamers also ran periodically to Port-Bail, it is not known if they carried mail.

From about 1873 the cutter L'ECHO carried mail between Guernsey and St. Malo and Brieux until she was wrecked in 1884. L'ECHO was followed by the dandy OENONE from 1885 until 1887.

A new company operated the Jersey to Carteret mail service from 1894, this was the Compagnie Rouenaise de Navigation, which was allied with the West of France Railway Company. One could in those days purchase a through ticket from the Jersey Eastern Railway office in Snow Hill, St. Helier direct to Paris.

PADDLE STEAMER 'CYGNE'

DISEMBARKING FROM THE 'CYGNE' AT GOREY C1895 NOTE H.M.S. RAVEN

The first paddle steamer used was the CYGNE which ran until 1913, when another paddle-ship the JERSEY (ex LORD NELSON) previously owned by the Great Yarmouth Tug Company was used. JERSEY was taken over by the Admiralty in the first world war, returning at the end of the war, and is out of records by 1920. A short note in the local newspaper of 1929 says: "Arrival of the new boat ROSE STAR for the Gorey to Carteret service." It is not known if she carried mail.

PADDLE STEAMER 'JERSEY'

A mail service also ran to St. Brieuc periodically with vessels of the Plymouth, Channel Islands & Brittany Steam Ship Company Limited. These were the COMMERCE, a Guernsey built steamer of 120 tons and the PLYMOUTH which ran twice weekly in 1888. The DEVONIA took over from the COMMERCE around the year 1900. The above company also carried mail between Jersey and Guernsey. I cannot trace DEVONIA in records after 1915. The ROSSGULL, another of the company's vessels foundered off St. Brelade in December, 1900 and the captain and crew were drowned.

In 1896 the London & South Western Railway placed the newly built VICTORIA (ibid) on the St. Malo to Jersey run, where she gave excellent service until 1919 when she was sold.

From 1919 until 1932 the Jersey to France service was operated by vessels of the Compagnie General Transatlantique with LA NYMPHE, ST. MALO, DINARD and ST. BRIEUC. The ST. MALO was lost off the Brayes rocks, Guernsey, in November, 1915, and is not to be confused with a vessel of the same name built for the L.S.W.R. Company in 1865.

ST. BRIEUC, under Captain Lasbliez, ended this company's service in May, 1932, when the Southern Railway Company took over, in June that year, with the VERA (ibid) until the

ST. BRIEUC

following year when the newly built BRITTANY came on the station, having been especially built for the Jersey to St. Malo service. At the commencement of W.W.II, the mail service to France from Jersey was discontinued, and although BRITTANY returned to her station after the war, has never been resumed. BRITTANY was withdrawn in 1963, sold to Finland and renamed ALANDSFARJAN.

QUEEN OF THE ISLES   J.M.Y. TROTTER

42

The Jersey Post Office
(Part II)

Meanwhile, at Jersey's post office the 21st February, 1816, saw the retirement of 82-year old Charles Le Geyt, Jersey's first postmaster. His son George William Le Geyt assumed the position of postmaster and continued at the original post office in Hue Street until 1827, when it was transferred to Minden Place.

On the 27th January, 1842, George William Le Geyt was dismissed from the post office service, due to pressure from his creditors, (probably owing to a local bank failure), he was replaced pro-tem by a Mr. Gardner until the new postmaster, Arthur Woodgate took over on the 17th February. Meanwhile Le Geyt had bolted from the island on the 13th February, and because he owned his own house which was the post office in Minden Place, another post office had to be found, this was the Old Parsonage or Deanery of St. Helier.

The following year on the 15th April, the post office was transferred again, this time to number 9 Bond Street, which was originally Jersey's Customs office and is now the main offices of British Rail. The new Postmaster, Lieutenant Robert Fullerton, took command on the same date.

The movements of the General Post office of Jersey were as follows:-

    1794–1827 HUE STREET.
    1827–1842 MINDEN PLACE.
    1842–1843 THE OLD PARSONAGE.
    1843–1852 BOND STREET.
    1852–1881 QUEEN STREET.
    1881–1909 HALKETT PLACE.
    1909–1971 BROAD STREET.
    1971–   MONT MILLAIS (Now the Post Office Headquarters.)

A few odd, but relevant, items turn up in the local newspapers of the period, but as only the scantiest details were given, they will be presented as written:-

"The coaches which carried passengers from the Weymouth packet station to their various destinations in the late 18th century were as follows:-

THE BEE to Salisbury.
THE ROYAL DORSET to Bristol.
The EMERALD & JOHN BULL to Bath.
The INDEPENDANT to Southampton on Tuesdays and Thursdays.
The DUKE of WELLINGTON to Southampton on Saturdays.

However, the one used by most Channel Islands passengers was the famous MAGNET mail coach which travelled from Weymouth to London via Melcombe Regis, Wareham, Lytchet Minster, Poole, Palmer's Ford, Ringwood, Romsey, Winchester, Alresford, Alton, Farnham, Frimley Bridge, Bagshot, Egham, Staines, Hounslow, Brentford via Kingston to the General Post Office in Lombard Street. The MAGNET coach station at Weymouth was the 'Golden Lion Inn.'

1822. Passengers travelling to Jersey this year from Southampton totalled 687.

1822. Up to the year ending the 5th January, 1823, the total expense to the General Post Office of the Weymouth packet station was £778 3s. 5d.

1837. The Admiralty orders:- 'All Captains of packets to wear cocked hats and swords in future.'

1837. An advertisement in the local paper:- 'Three shillings per week will be paid to a man armed with cutlass and pistols, to guard the mail in transit from the Jersey post office to the packets in the harbour.

1837. Two additional letter carriers authorised for St. Helier and three penny post carriers, increasing the carriers from five to ten, each to be paid from 5 to 6 shillings per week.

1839. 5,212, passengers carried by the Weymouth packets this year.

1843. The law was passed in Jersey making street naming and house numbering compulsory.

1844. The General Post Office of London, publishes a caution to masters of vessels arriving in Jersey, to take their letter bags to the post office and not deliver them privately in town. Penalty £5 for every letter delivered.

1852. March. A post office is to be built in Queen Street, Jersey, on the site of Mr. Balcam's house, destroyed by fire, opposite to Gibsons Hotel.

1852. April. The General post office is applying for a mail carrier between Trinity and St. Helier, through St. Martin, Gorey and St. Clement. The bags may be carried on horseback, in a close covered mail cart or by omnibus. The carrier must do seven miles per hour stoppages included.

1852. 23rd November. The first letter boxes erected in the United Kingdom were in the Channel Islands, those at Jersey were placed in David Place, New Street, Cheapside and St. Clement's Road. This was done at the instance of Anthony Trollope the famous novelist, who was at the time a post office surveyor and whose district encompassed the Channel Islands.

1860. November. Jersey's postmen appear in uniform for the first time.

1885. 29th September. Arrival of the first carrier pigeon from the Isle of Wight with news for the 'British Press' (newspaper) (Jersey's first airmail?)

Adhesive postage stamps were unknown until May, 1840, when the famous 'Penny Black' was issued. Up until then the Jersey post office had first used the name of the Island in a concave curve as a handstamp, from 1794 to 1799. The second handstamp was of two types 'JERSEY' in a straight line in use from 1797 to 1810, the name 'JERSEY' in a scroll form was used up to 1830.

Further detailed information on early Channel Islands postal history, may be obtained from the publications of the 'Channel Islands Specialists Society.'

An event of great significance took place on the 1st October, 1969, when the States of Jersey and Guernsey assumed responsibility for the operation of the Islands postal services from Her Majesty's Postmaster-General. In Jersey the appointments of Head Postmaster and Assistant Head Postmaster were abolished, they were replaced by a Director of the Department of Postal Administration and two controllers.

British postage stamps are now invalid as the Islands have their own issues which are avidly sought after by philatelists all over the world, philatelic bureaux have been established in the Islands to cater for their needs.

The wind of change is also effecting the Head post office in Broad Street, St. Helier as from early in 1971 letter sorting operations will be transferred to the new Jersey Postal Administrations building and now the headquarters at Mont Millais, the alterations have cost £230,000. Jersey postmen have also been issued with new style uniforms.

The London & South Western Railway Company (Part II)

BRITTANY

The next new L.S.W.R. Company's vessel following the NORMANDY was the BRITTANY which was an iron paddle steamer of 525 tons, built for the company by J. Ash & Company of Cubitt Town. She had engines by J. Stewart of Poplar developing 250 h.p. and a speed of 14 knots, her cargo capacity was 250 tons. BRITTANY's maiden voyage to Jersey was on the 17th November, 1864, under Captain Goodridge who had commanded the DISPATCH. BRITTANY was lengthened in 1873 and was then of 678 tons. She ran for many years between Southampton and the Channel Islands and was finally sold to Preston shipbreakers in 1900. BRITTANY was the last paddle ship built for the L.S.W.R. Company.

PADDLE STEAMER 'BRITTANY'

ON BOARD THE PADDLE STEAMER 'BRITTANY'

SCREW STEAMER 'GRIFFIN'

47

GRIFFIN

1865 saw the GRIFFIN purchased from a Mr. Beard a Scottish ironmaster. One report stated that the GRIFFIN was the first iron screw steamer to come to Jersey, and was used mainly between Jersey and France. In August, 1876, she was badly damaged whilst on a voyage from Southampton to St. Malo, she was run into by the steam tug SOVEREIGN, GRIFFIN was beached on the Itchen shore and later towed to Southampton for repairs. On the 5th July, 1878, GRIFFIN brought Victor Hugo and his family to Jersey, where they stayed for some time, the family later moved to Guernsey. GRIFFIN was sold in 1895 and was lost in the West Indies c 1900.

SCREW STEAMER 'ST. MALO'

ST. MALO

The ST. MALO was built for the London & South Western Railway Company's Southampton to St. Malo service in 1865 by Aitken & Mansell of Glasgow, and was the first iron single screw steamer built by them of 610 tons, she had a straight stem. In 1866 she was running twice per week between the Channel Islands and Southampton and later ran from the C.I. and France, in about 1899 some of her passenger accommodation was removed to give more cargo space. ST. MALO was sold in 1905 to J. Power & Company for £300 who in turn sold her to Dutch shipbreakers in 1906.

CAESAREA

1867 saw the building of the ill fated CAESAREA for the L.S.W.R. Company. The first of three vessels of the same name, she was an iron single screw steamer of 282 tons, built by Aitken & Mansell of Glasgow for the Channel Islands mail service, she ran for seventeen years also going to France and it was on a voyage to St. Malo on the 27th June, 1884, that she collided with the S.S. STRATHESK in fog, twelve miles off Cap De La Hague and was wrecked.

PADDLE STEAMER 'WAVERLEY'

WRECK OF THE 'WAVERLEY' OFF GUERNSEY, 1873. THE 'DISPATCH' STANDING BY
FROM A PAINTING BY P. OULESS IN THE POSSESSION OF MISS OULESS 1967.
PHOTO GIVEN TO R. MAYNE BY MR. PORTER

WAVERLEY
In August 1868, the L. & S.W.R. Company bought an iron paddle steamer the WAVERLEY

from the North British Railway Company. WAVERLEY had been built in 1865, by A. & J. Inglis of Glasgow of 529 tons and 222 feet in length her engines developed 280 h.p. Her lounge was fitted with coloured glass scenes of Sir Walter Scott's novels. WAVERLEY had originally ran between Silloth and Dublin and was also used as a blockade runner during the American civil war, she was refitted at Northam and placed on the Channel Islands to Southampton mail run in 1868. On the 5th June, 1873, on a voyage from Southampton, WAVERLEY struck the Platte Bou rock off Guernsey and was wrecked, fortunately without loss of life. The mail was taken to Guernsey the same day by the BRITTANY and later the Jersey mail was brought over by the DASHER the old mail ship which was then a fishery protection vessel. There was an enquiry but WAVERLEY's captain, Captain Mabb, was exonerated.

PADDLE STEAMER 'HAVRE'

HAVRE

1870 saw the appearance in the Channel Islands of another L.S.W.R. Company mailship, the iron paddle steamer HAVRE, which was built in 1856 by Ditchburn & Mare of Blackwall. Of 517 tons, 184 feet in length, a 24 foot beam, a depth of 14 foot 6 inches. Her engines were Seward three cylinder atmospheric developing 220 h.p. which drove her 21 foot diameter paddle wheels, the vessel achieving a speed of 13 knots. HAVRE was reputed to be the smallest and most uncomfortable steamer on the station. On a voyage from Southampton to the Islands on the 16th February, 1875, HAVRE struck the Platte Bou rocks off Guernsey and was wrecked, the passengers and crew were rescued and the mails saved and taken to Guernsey by the HONFLEUR. At a subsequent enquiry HAVRE's captain, Captain Long was suspended for twelve months.

WRECK OF THE 'HAVRE' OFF GUERNSEY 16—2—1875

ALICE 1871—1888

ALICE and the FANNIE

Two beautiful iron paddle steamers which were purchased by the London & South Western
Railway Company in 1870 were the ALICE and the FANNIE, built in 1859 by Laird of
Greenock, of 635 tons, 231 feet in length with a 26 foot beam, they had two funnels and a

clipper bow. ALICE ran to the channel islands periodically with mail, until converted to a hulk in 1888 and scrapped in 1898. FANNIE commenced running to the islands in 1870, but was mainly on the Southampton to Havre station, in 1878 she was carrying cattle being finally sold in 1887 and most authorities state broken up in 1890.

'HONFLEUR'

HONFLEUR
A vessel built for the Channel Islands to France service was the HONFLEUR, built by Aitken & Mansel in 1873, for the L.S.W.R. Company, of 429 tons, she was a single screw steamer with a speed of 11½ knots and commanded by Captain Frank Allix, her normal run being from Jersey to Granville with passengers, mail and cargo. HONFLEUR was sold in 1911, to a Mr. Gailbraith of Glasgow for £900 and in 1930 was owned by a company in Constantinople.

GUERNSEY
The single screw steamer GUERNSEY followed in 1874. Built for the L.S.W.R. Company by J. & W. Dudgeon of Blackwall, of 572 tons and a speed of 13 knots, GUERNSEY was commanded by Captain Du Feu, her regular run was Southampton to the Channel Islands, but she also ran to France. In November, 1903, she was in collision of St. Catherine, Jersey and in December, 1913, she struck a rock off Roscoff and was seriously damaged. GUERNSEY was later converted to cargo carrying only and eventually wrecked off Cap De La Hague on the 9th April, 1915, there being no light in operation as a wartime measure, seven of the crew were drowned.

GUERNSEY

SOUTH-WESTERN

SOUTH WESTERN
The SOUTH WESTERN, second vessel of that name on local service, was built for the

L.S.W.R. Company by J. & W. Dudgeon of Blackwall in 1874, she was an iron single screw steamer of 674 tons and had a speed of 13 knots. Her first voyage to Jersey was on the 30th March, 1875, she had a somewhat eventful career, colliding with a Norwegian barque in December, 1881, damaged in collision with the BAY FISHER in July, 1893, SOUTH WESTERN was the first of the company's ships to have radio fitted as an experiment in December, 1910, whilst on the Southampton to Cherbourg route. SOUTH WESTERN was on a voyage to St. Malo on March the 16th, 1918, when she was torpedoed by a German submarine and lost.

'DIANA'

DIANA
In 1876 the L.S.W.R. Company had the DIANA built by Aitken & Mansel of Whiteinch, she was a single screw steamer of 850 tons, 232 feet in length, her 200 h.p. engines giving a speed of 14 knots. Her service was mainly from Southampton to the Channel Islands, DIANA also ran from Southampton to St. Malo and whilst on that service on the 21st June, 1895, she struck rocks in the Little Russel passage off Guernsey and was wrecked. The passengers and crew were saved but the mails were lost. Her commander, Captain Kemp, had his certificate suspended for six months and his chief officer was reprimanded.

WRECK OF THE 'CALEDONIA' IN 1881

CALEDONIA

The CALEDONIA formerly the HOGARTH, was an iron single screw steamer built by Conliffe & Dunlop at Port Glasgow in 1876, of 355 tons and a speed of 14 knots, she was purchased by the L.S.W.R. Company in 1878, chiefly for the Southampton to St. Malo trade, but in consequence of the FANNIE being repaired, CALEDONIA ran to the Channel Islands under the command of Captain Lainson with John Winter as chief mate. On a voyage from Guernsey to Jersey on the 19th February, 1881, at 6.00 a.m. CALEDONIA struck the Oyster Rock just outside of St. Helier harbour and sank, all passengers and crew were saved. The mails were salvaged by divers and taken to the Jersey General Post Office, where they were dried out and delivered the following day, Sunday. CALEDONIA's engines were raised on the 11th July, 1881.

ELLA

ELLA was built for the L.S.W.R. Company in 1881 by Aitken & Mansel of Whiteinch for the Southampton to Cherbourg run, but came to the Channel Islands periodically. An iron single screw steamer of 851 tons with a speed of 14 knots, ELLA had a straight stem, one funnel and two masts. Her first voyage to Jersey was on the 31st July, 1881, under the command of Captain Merrels, she carried 238 passengers. ELLA was sold to the shipping federation in 1913 and was eventually broken up in 1926.

HILDA

1882 saw the building of the HILDA by Aitken & Mansel of Whiteinch, for the L.S.W.R.

'ELLA'

Company, an iron single screw steamer of 849 tons, 235 feet in length, 29 foot breadth and 14 foot in depth, her 220 h.p. engines gave her a speed of 14 knots. HILDA could carry 234 passengers, her normal service was Southampton to C.I. to St. Malo and her maiden voyage to Jersey was on the 19th January, 1883, On the 18th November, 1905, during a blizzard HILDA struck the Roche du Jardin Rock off the Isle of Cezembre, St. Malo and was wrecked with the fearful loss of one hundred and twenty eight lives, all her crew including Captain Gregory were lost except for one fortunate sailor. The mails were also lost. A French company issued a set of postcards showing the wreck, a more macabre photograph of the time shows the dead Captain Gregory in close up as he was laid on a straw strewn floor.

LAURA

The first steel built vessel for the L.S.W.R. Company was the LAURA built by Aitken & Mansel of Whiteinch, in 1885 a screw steamer of 641 tons, she had a single funnel and two masts. LAURA was built to replace the CAESAREA on the Southampton to C.I. to France run, and commenced service in 1885. After about thirty years uneventful service and being transferred to cargo carrying only, LAURA was sold and was eventually lost in a hurricane off the Bahamas whilst bootlegging.

SAINT-MALO - Naufrage du " Hilda "
(19 Novembre 1905)
Scaphandriers à la recherche des Victimes G. F.
SAINT-MALO - Shipwreck of the " Hilda "
(November 19th 1905)
Divers searching for the victims

WRECK OF THE 'HILDA' 1905

WRECK OF THE 'HILDA' 1905

CAPTAIN GREGORY OF THE 'HILDA'

6 OF THE SURVIVORS OF THE WRECKED 'HILDA'

LAURA

The Great Rivals, L.S.W.R. and G.W.R.

In 1889 the Great Western Railway Company bought out the Weymouth & Channel Islands Steam Packet Company and ran their own ships. Then an agreement was formed whereby the Great Western Railway Company and the London & South Western Railway Company pooled all Channel Islands mail traffic.

GAEL

From Weymouth in 1889 came the GAEL which ran for only six months to the C.I. She was a paddle steamer built by Robertson & Company of Greenock in 1867, of 354 tons, 211 feet in length with a 23 foot beam, having two funnels and two masts, she was engined by Rankin & Blackmore of Greenock, and was originally built for the Campbeltown & Glasgow Steam Packet Company, GAEL was sold to the G.W.R. Company in 1884, in 1889 she was sold to David McBrayne of Glasgow and used in the highlands. GAEL was sold again in 1891, and eventually broken up in 1922.

GREAT WESTERN

The GREAT WESTERN was built in 1867, by W. Simons & Company of Renfrew for the G.W.R. Company's Irish service, a 447 ton paddle steamer 220 feet in length with a 25 foot beam. GREAT WESTERN was loaned to the Weymouth & Channel Islands Steam Packet Company for six months in 1887, to replace the wrecked BRIGHTON. The GREAT WESTERN was sold in 1891 to David McBrayne of Glasgow and re-named LOVEDALE she was broken up in 1905.

LYNX

The first of the G.W.R. Company's newly built ships was the LYNX, built by Laird Brothers of Birkenhead, at a cost of £35,000 she was a steel twin screw steamer, like her two sister ships the ANTELOPE and GAZELLE, of 609 tons and a speed of 18 knots. Her maiden voyage to Jersey was on the 1st August, 1889, in 1914 the LYNX as H.M.S. LYNN captured the ANTELOPE (her sister ship) in the mediterranean carrying contraband. Two of her many commanders were Captain W. Rumsey, appointed on 18th May, 1896, and Captain Allen. In 1912 the LYNX was converted to cargo and was eventually sold and broken up in 1925.

'LYNX'

G.W.R. CAPTAINS PAINTER & RUMSEY ON THE 'LYNX'

STEWARDESS AND CAPTAIN PAINTER ON THE LYNX

ANTELOPE

ANTELOPE

The second of the trio of new ships LYNX, ANTELOPE and GAZELLE built for the G.W.R. Company by Laird Bros. of Birkenhead and costing £35,000 each, came to Jersey on the 3rd August 1889, this was the ANTELOPE, a steel twin screw steamer of 609 tons, her engines developed a speed of 16 knots. ANTELOPE was only used occasionally on the C.I. run after 1900, because then her normal run was between Plymouth and Brest, she was sold in August, 1913, to a Greek firm and re-named ATROMITOS, as the ATROMITOS she was captured in the mediterranean in 1914 whilst carrying contraband by her sister ship the LYNX then under the admiralty as H.M.S. LYNN. The ATROMITOS (ex ANTE-LOPE) was still in service in 1930.

GAZELLE

GAZELLE

The third member of this famous trio was the GAZELLE, which first came to Jersey on the 8th September, 1889, she did the mail run for nineteen years being converted to cargo carrying in 1908. GAZELLE was sold by the Great Western Railway Company in 1925 after thirty six years service, and broken up.

GAZELLE AS A CARGO SHIP AFTER 1908

'DORA'

DORA

Meanwhile the London & South Western Railway Company was not idle, for on the 26th May, 1889, they put on service the newly built DORA. She was built by R. Napier & Sons of Glasgow, and launched at Govan in March, 1889, a single screw steamer of 820 tons with a speed of 16 knots. DORA was the first of the L.S.W.R. Company's fleet to be lighted by electricity. On the 16th May, 1893, whilst outgoing from Jersey she struck a rock off of Guernsey, DORA was towed to St. Peter Port by the LYNX and her passengers and mails were landed in boats, her commander, Captain Nutbeam was severely censured. DORA having been repaired continued for another eight years on the Southampton to C.I. run being sold to the Isle of Man Steam Packet Company in 1901, being re-named DOUGLAS and in 1923 she was involved in a collision in the Mersey and was lost.

FREDERICA

FREDERICA

The L.S.W.R. Company had three sister ships built to combat those of the G.W.R. Company's LYNX, GAZELLE and ANTELOPE. These three new vessels were named FREDERICA, LYDIA and STELLA. They were built for the company by J. & G. Thomson of Clydebank in 1890, of 1,059 tons each they were twin screw steel steamers. The FREDERICA first came to Jersey on the 31st July, 1890, a splendid vessel with reciprocating engines giving a speed of 19½ knots, she had a single funnel which was lengthened in 1904 and had the lower moulding removed, in the early days her davits were painted black. In 1911 FREDERICA was sold to a Turkish company and renamed NILUFER, she was finally lost in the 1914–1918 war. For many years on local service she was commanded by that well known Jerseyman Captain George Allix.

LYDIA

Following the FREDERICA on the 7th October, 1890, came the LYDIA her sister ship, at that time the fastest vessel in existence her speed being 24½ statute miles per hour, her record being broken the following year when the Great Western Railway Company put on their new vessel the IBEX. Before 1902 LYDIA only had one mast and in 1904 she was altered and improved, her after end was plated instead of staunchions and two steel lifeboats were fitted on her after deck instead of the one which had been on the starboard side. In 1919, LYDIA was sold to the Coast Lines company running from Dublin to Preston, and later she was resold to a Greek company and renamed IERAX she was broken up in 1937.

64

Among her many commanders were Captains Allix, Darnell, A.H. Stride and Vanderplank.

CAPTAIN LAINSON

CAPTAIN VANDERPLANK

CAPTAIN ALLIX

CAPTAIN FRANCIS J. RENOUF

65

LYDIA

LYDIA AND FREDERICA

'STELLA'

STELLA

The third of the L.S.W.R. Company's trio of sisters was the ill-fated STELLA whose maiden voyage to Jersey was on the 6th November, 1890, unfortunately only eight and a half years passed until on a voyage from Southampton to Guernsey at 4.10 p.m. on the 30th March 1899, STELLA struck the Black Rock on the Casquets reef and was wrecked with the terrible loss of 105 lives; 46 passengers were rescued by the LYNX, 64 by the VERA, a french tugboat took 6 passengers and 3 seamen off a floating pantechnicon and landed them at Cherbourg. In Liverpool Cathederal there is a memorial window panel devoted to 'Noble Women' and one depicts Mrs. Mary Rogers the stewardess of the STELLA who gave her lifebelt to a passenger, refused a place in the lifeboat and was drowned.

During the comparatively short life of the STELLA her various commanders were Captains Heathcote, Lainson and Captain Riggs who went down with his vessel.

IBEX

The Great Western Railway Company not to be outdone by the fast new vessels of the rival L.S.W.R. Company and especially their LYDIA, had the IBEX built in 1891, by Laird Brothers of Birkenhead. A steel twin screw steamer schooner rigged, of 1,160 gross tons, 265 feet in length, with a 32½ foot beam and had two masts and two funnels, she carried 600 passengers and had sleeping accommodation for 210. IBEX first came to Jersey on the 5th September, 1891, and it was not long before she broke the speed record set up by

THE 'IBEX'

the LYDIA of the L.S.W.R. Company. However, IBEX did not go unscathed for in 1897 she struck the Noirmontaise Rock off Jersey whilst racing the FREDERICA and tore a hole 10 feet by 2 feet. Her 230 passengers were landed at Portelet Bay and the next day IBEX was towed to St. Aubin's fort and St. Helier the day after by the REINDEER. At a later enquiry her commander, Captain John Le Feuvre was suspended for six months. Captain John Le Feuvre had been appointed only a few months before in May, 1896. On the 5th January, 1900, IBEX again struck a rock off Platte Fougere, Guernsey, and sank with a loss of two lives, Captain Baudains was suspended for six months, she was refloated months later, repaired and placed back on service. On the 18th April, 1914, IBEX collided with a disabled schooner the HANNAH CROASDALE off Portland and on the 19th September, 1917, she collided with, and sank, the Great Western Railway cargo steamer ALETTA twenty miles off Weymouth, all the crew were saved. IBEX was replaced by the ST. JULIEN and broken up in 1926–7 after a most eventful life.

CAPTAIN JOHN LE FEUVRE (CENTRE) AND TWO OFFICERS ON THE 'IBEX'

ALMA

69

ALMA and COLUMBIA (sister ships)

In 1894 the London & South Western Railway Company had the sister ships ALMA and COLUMBIA built by J. & G. Thomson of Clydebank for the Southampton to Havre service. They were twin screw steamers of 1,145 tons, their engines developed 3,300 I.H.P. at a speed of 19 knots. These two vessels were the first cross channel steamers to be fitted with small two berth cabins for first class passengers. They called occasionally at the Channel Islands and were eventually both sold in 1912 to a Senor Sitges of Algiers.

COLUMBIA

VICTORIA

The next ship built for the L.S.W.R. Company's Jersey to France service was the screw steamer VICTORIA, built in 1896 by J. & G. Thomson of Clydebank. VICTORIA's maiden voyage to the Channel Islands was on the 25th July, 1896, to supplement the ALLIANCE on the Jersey to St. Malo run under the command of Captain A. Jones. Another of her commanders at a later date was Captain Du Feu. VICTORIA was sold in 1919.

VICTORIA

ROEBUCK and REINDEER (sister ships)
Two famous Great Western Railway Company's ships were the sisters ROEBUCK and
REINDEER. Built in 1897 by the Naval Construction & Armament Company of Barrow, of
1,093 tons, 280 feet in length with a beam of 35 feet 5 inches, they were schooner rigged
twin screw steamers with reciprocating engines developing a speed of 20 knots.

REINDEER AND ROEBUCK AT JERSEY

ROEBUCK's maiden voyage to Jersey was on the 1st July, 1897. She was licensed to carry 842 passengers. On the 26th January, 1905, she caught fire at New Milford, in 1908 she caught fire in the channel. In July, 1911, on a voyage from Jersey to Guernsey and Weymouth, she struck the Kaines Rocks near St. Brelades and was eventually beached on St. Brelade's Bay where she remained until towed to St. Helier's harbour. All aboard were rescued including 104 passengers, and the mails were also salvaged, from St. Helier ROEBUCK was towed to Southampton for repair, her master was suspended for six months, in 1914 ROEBUCK was sold to the Government and renamed ROEDEAN and whilst in the Scapa Flow on January 13th, 1915, she broke her moorings in a storm, rammed the battleship L'IMPERIEUSE, ROEDEAN stove in her bows and sank in five fathoms of water. Captain L.T. Richardson of the ST. JULIEN noted that her ribs were still visible in 1941.

REINDEER appeared to have a less eventful life than her sister, she had her trials on the Clyde in June, 1897, and her maiden voyage to Jersey was on the 2nd August the same year. REINDEER had her funnel bonnets removed in 1903 and was damaged in 1926 when she struck Jersey's Albert pier and had to go to Plymouth for repair. From 1925 she had been on cargo service. REINDEER was sold for scrap in 1928. The various commanders of these two vessels were Captains Vine, Le Feuvre, Langdon and Mulhall.

ARRIVAL OF JERSEY BOAT, WEYMOUTH.

THE 'ROEBUCK' AT WEYMOUTH C1905

10 *JERSEY. — St-Hélier. — Guernesey-Boat leaving St-Hélier.* —{LL.

ROEBUCK

REINDEER

DAMAGE TO ROEBUCK ON THE KAINES ROCKS 1911

ROEBUCK BEACHED AT ST. BRELADE

VERA

VERA'S DINING SALOON

VERA

VERA first came to the Channel Islands in October, 1898. A twin screw steamer with reciprocating engines the VERA was built for the L. & S.W.R. Company in 1898, by the Clydebank Engineering Shipbuilding Company, she was of 1,008 tons, and had a speed of 19½ knots. VERA was damaged in collision with the SIMLA in Southampton water on the 22nd March, 1901, during the 1914—18 war she sank a German U-Boat by gunfire off the Isle of Wight. In 1932 VERA was refitted, transferred and opened the Jersey to St. Malo service when the Southern Railway Company took over from the France to Jersey Line the following year VERA was sold and broken up. Her two known commanders were Captains Withers and Smith. Captain Smith was Fleet Commodore Captain after Captain Allix (ALBERTA).

ALBERTA

ALBERTA

The ALBERTA was built to replace the ill fated STELLA for the L.S.W.R. Company in 1900 by John Brown and was a twin screw steamer of 1,193 tons with reciprocating engines giving a speed of 19½ knots. ALBERTA's maiden voyage to Jersey was on the 2nd June, 1900, in July, 1920, she struck a rock near Guernsey and reached St. Peter Port leaking and with a list, she was taken out of commission in 1929 after completing 75,000 miles and carrying 700,000 passengers, ALBERTA was sold to a Greek company in 1930. Her various commanders were Captains Allix, Winter, Carter, Smith and Howe. She was renamed in 1934 MYKALI, and in 1935 reverted to her name ALBERTA, in 1941 she was bombed and sunk at Salamis.

GREAT SOUTHERN   E. LATCHEM, WEYMOUTH

GREAT WESTERN   E. LATCHEM, WEYMOUTH

GREAT WESTERN and GREAT SOUTHERN (sister ships)
Two of the G.W.R. Company's vessels which could only be described as relief packets to
the Channel Islands were the GREAT WESTERN and the GREAT SOUTHERN. Sister ships
built by Laird of Birkenhead in 1902, they were twin screw steamers of 1,224 tons, built
originally for the Waterford to Milford service, they came to the Islands in peak periods
only, they were sold for breaking in 1933 and 1934 respectively.

PRINCESS ENA

PRINCESS ENA

The PRINCESS ENA was built for the L. & S.W.R. Company's Southampton to St. Malo trade, calling at the Channel Islands in the early days on excursions and cruises only, but she did carry mail from Jersey on occasions. Built in four months by Gourlay Brothers of Dundee in 1906 of 1,198 tons, 250 feet in length and a breadth of 33 feet, she was a twin screw turbine steamer. On the 19th May, 1908, PRINCESS ENA struck the Paternoster Rocks off Jersey and reached St. Helier the next day in a disabled condition. On the 13th August, 1923, whilst on a voyage from Southampton to St. Malo she struck the Minquiers Rocks, but managed to limp into St. Malo harbour. The final incident occured on the 3rd August, 1935, when on a voyage from Jersey to St. Malo the PRINCESS ENA caught fire off Corbiere, Jersey, burned out and sank, all passengers and crew being rescued and taken off by the ST. JULIEN. The mails were also saved.

CAESAREA and SARNIA (sister ships)

Two famous L. & S.W.R. Company's sister ships (the second pair of ships with these names) still remembered by many people were the CAESAREA and the SARNIA named after the alleged Roman names for Jersey and Guernsey. Built in 1910 by Cammel Laird & Company of Birkenhead at a cost of £75,000 each, they were triple screw turbine steamers of 1,505 tons, 284 feet in length with a 39 foot breadth and had a speed of 20½ knots. They each carried 980 passengers, and were the first triple turbine steamers on the Channel Islands run.

CAESAREA

CAESAREA 20th OF JULY, 1923

CAESAREA first came to Jersey on the 26th September, 1910, under the command of Captain Winter and the old crew of the ALBERTA and carrying 980 passengers, she gave excellent service for thirteen years until the 7th July, 1923, when she struck a rock off Noirmont Point, Jersey and in returning to St. Helier struck the Oyster Rock (so often the demise of many a fine ship) and sank just outside the harbour mouth, fortunately without incurring loss of life she was refloated and sent to England for repair, the HANTONIA taking over her service in July. The same year CAESAREA was sold to the Isle of Man Steam Packet Company and renamed MANX MAID she was engaged in Admiralty work during the 1939—45 war and was eventually sold and broken up in 1950.

CAESAREA OUTSIDE ST. HELIER HARBOUR

SARNIA

The SARNIA first came to Jersey on the 13th April, 1911 and was used during the 1914—18 war as an armed boarding vessel on service in the mediterranean until the 12th September, 1918, when she was torpedoed and sunk by a German U-Boat.

ARDENA

The ARDENA (ex PEONY) was built in 1915 by A. Macmillan & Son of Dumbarton as H.M. Escort vessel PEONY she was purchased and converted by the L. & S.W.R. Company in 1920 for the Southampton to France service, a single screw steamer of 1,092 tons and a speed of 16 knots, she occasionally ran to the Channel Islands with passengers and mail during peak periods. ARDENA was sold out of service in 1934.

RATHMORE and GALTEEMORE

These two vessels the RATHMORE and the GALTEEMORE were Irish cargo screw steamers on charter to the London & South Western Railway Company for service which included carrying mail to the Channel Islands during the 1914—18 war.

MELLIFONT

This Great Western Railway Company's cargo boat brought the mail to the Channel Islands in June, 1915.

NORMANNIA

NORMANNIA and HANTONIA (sister ships)

Two L. & S.W.R. Company's sister ships which could only be described as relief ships, as their normal route was from Southampton to Le Havre were the NORMANNIA and the HANTONIA. Built in 1911 by the Fairfield Shipbuilding & Engineering Company at Govan, they were twin screw, coal steam turbines of 1,560 tons gross, they were 290 feet in length and 36 feet in breadth, their engines developed 4,750 h.p. giving a speed of 18 knots.

NORMANNIA first came to Jersey in 1912, she was lost during the second world war being bombed and sunk by German aircraft at Dunkirk in 1940.

HANTONIA   BRITISH RAIL

HANTONIA first came to Jersey to relieve the CAESAREA which was damaged in July, 1923. She served as an accommodation vessel during the second world war. After the war she operated the C.I. to Southampton service for about 18 months and was ultimately broken up at Grays, Essex in June, 1952.

LORINA
The LORINA was built in 1918, by Denny of Dumbarton for the L. & S.W.R. Company. She was a twin screw turbine steamer of 1,578 tons, 300 feet in length, she had a speed of 19½ knots, her first twelve months were spent in carrying troops across the channel, after which she was re-fitted and passed to her owners in 1919. LORINA first came to Jersey on the 1st April, 1920. On the 23rd September, 1935, after leaving St. Helier she struck a rock in the small roads and was badly damaged below the waterline. LORINA was sunk by German bombers at Dunkirk in 1940 with the NORMANNIA. Captain Light was commander of the LORINA for several years.

DINARD and ST. BRIAC (sister ships)
The DINARD and the ST. BRIAC were built by Denny of Dumbarton in 1924, being sister ships each of 2,291 tons, 325 feet in length, 41 feet in breadth, they were twin screw

LORINA

steam turbines with a speed of 19½ knots. Built mainly for the Southampton to St. Malo service they came to Jersey at peak periods, and were also used for cruises they could carry 1,340 passengers.

DINARD

DINARD served as a hospital ship during World War II, after which she was converted in 1947 to a car ferry, enabling her to carry 300 passengers and 80 cars on the Dover to Boulogne route, DINARD was withdrawn in October, 1958, and sold to Finland in 1959, being re-named VIKING.

ST. BRIAC

ST. BRIAC was not so fortunate for during her service in World War II, on the 13th March, 1942, she struck a mine off Aberdeen and was lost.

ST. HELIER and ST. JULIEN (sister ships)
In 1925 the Great Western Railway Company had the two well known sister ships the ST. HELIER and the ST. JULIEN built by John Brown & Company of Clydebank. They were each of 1,950 gross tons, twin screw steam turbines developing a speed of 18 knots, they were 291 feet in length, with a 40 foot beam.

ST. HELIER was launched on the 26th March, 1925, and first came to Jersey on the 17th June, she was altered in 1928 and a funnel was removed. ST. HELIER was taken over by the Royal Navy in November 1940, and saw service at Calais and Dunkirk under Operation

ST. HELIER JERSEY EVENING POST

ST. JULIEN JERSEY EVENING POST

Dynamo which was the evacuation of the British Expeditionary force, she brought out 10,200 troops from Dunkirk and also 1,500 refugees, her guns shot down a German aircraft that attempted to bomb her. ST. HELIER was also at the Invasion, landing Canadian troops on the famous 6th June, 1944. Her Captain, R.R. Pitman who was Commodore of the whole of the British Railways Fleet was awarded the Distinguished Service Cross, he retired in 1959. ST. HELIER returned to the Channel Islands service in June 1946, she was sold in 1960, and her final trip from Jersey via Guernsey to Weymouth was on the 12th September. The ST. HELIER was scrapped in 1961 by Belgian shipbreakers. Her first commander was Captain Mulhall then Captain H. Walker but Captain R.R. Pitman, D.S.C., M.B.E. was her master from April, 1930, to April, 1959. Her final master was Captain H. Walker.

ST. JULIEN first came to Jersey on the 24th May, 1925, she was altered in 1929 and had one funnel removed. She served as a hospital ship during the Second World War, and evacuated troops from Dunkirk, Boulogne and Cherbourg. ST. JULIEN was sent to the mediterranean in 1943 and was at the Anzio landing in 1944, after which she was sent back to prepare for D Day. On D Day plus one she struck a mine but managed to limp into port. The ST. JULIEN resumed her station after the war, and her last voyage from Jersey was on the 27th September, 1960. She was broken up at the yard of Van Heyghen Freres at Ghent in Belgium in 1961.

Her various commanders were Captains C.H. Langdon, who died on board in 1927, J. Goodchild (ex second mate), Mulhall, L.T. Richardson (for 25 years), R.R. Pitman, D.S.C., M.B.E., and Victor Newton.

ST. PATRICK

DAMAGE TO ST. PATRICK 5—8—1932

ST. PATRICK

In 1930 the ST. PATRICK was built by Alex, Stephen & Sons of Glasgow for the Fishguard & Rosslare Railways & Harbours Company, but she came to the Channel Islands in peak periods. She was a twin screw turbine steamer of 1,922 tons, and a speed of 19 knots, she first came to Jersey on the 18th April, 1930. On the 5th August, 1932, ST. PATRICK struck the Frouquie Rock off La Moye, Jersey in fog and was badly damaged. Her passengers were taken off by the ISLE OF SARK and ST. PATRICK was towed to St. Helier. Her captain was censured and fined. On the 13th June, 1941, whilst nearing Fishguard from Rosslare on her regular run she was bombed by a German aircraft. The ST. PATRICK broke in half and disappeared in six minutes with the loss of 80 lives, following this action the stewardess was awarded the George Medal, and the second engineer and radio officer were awarded the M.B.E.

Vessels of The Southern Railway, British Transport Commission & British Railways

ISLE OF JERSEY and ISLE OF GUERNSEY (sister ships)

Denny Brothers of Dumbarton built the ISLE OF JERSEY and the ISLE OF GUERNSEY for the Southern Railway Company in 1930. These two sister ships were each of 2,143 tons, twin screw steam turbines, 306 feet in length with a 42 foot beam and a speed of 19½ knots.

ISLE OF JERSEY

The ISLE OF JERSEY first came to Jersey on the 13th March, 1931, under Captain Holt. During the war she served as a naval hospital ship and made eleven crossings to the invasion beaches, resuming her station after the war. She made her final voyage from Jersey on the 31st October, 1959, amid the salutations of all the sirens, hooters and whistles from the other vessels in the harbour as is the custom. The ISLE OF JERSEY was refitted at Newcastle in 1960 and sold to Mr. M.S. Giaber of Tripoli, she was renamed LIBDA and commenced running between Benghazi and Tripoli under an Indian captain and was registered in Bombay. Broken up in 1963

ISLE OF GUERNSEY   JERSEY EVENING POST

The ISLE OF GUERNSEY made her maiden voyage to Jersey on the 5th April, 1931. During the second world war she was converted to a hospital ship and during 'Operation Dynamo' the evacuation of the B.E.F. from Dunkirk made trips to the beaches bringing back 836 wounded men. She was re-fitted as an L.C.I. for D Day and was the second vessel to enter Arromanches. The ISLE OF GUERNSEY resumed her regular service from Southampton on the 25th June, 1945, and eventually made her last voyage from Southampton to the Channel Islands in May, 1961, when Southampton was closed as a Channel Island passenger port, but ran from Weymouth to the Channel Islands until June, 1961. The ISLE OF GUERNSEY was sold to Van Heygen Freres the Belgian shipbreakers in November, 1961. Some of her commanders were Captains T.N. Darnell (retired 1933), Hill, Francis Trout and F. Cantle.

ISLE OF SARK   JERSEY EVENING POST

ISLE OF SARK

The ISLE OF SARK was built for the Southern Railway Company in 1932 by Denny Brothers for Channel Islands. A twin screw steam turbine of 2,211 tons, 306 feet in length, a beam of 42 feet and a speed of 19½ knots, she had a maierform stem and was the first vessel ever to be fitted with the famous Denny-Brown stabilizers of the type which were fitted in the Atlantic liners QUEEN MARY and QUEEN ELIZABETH. The ISLE OF SARK was the last vessel to evacuate the Channel Islands being actually in Guernsey during the air raid, which was followed by the German occupation. She was then placed on the Fishguard to Rosslare service until taken over by the Admiralty and used as a Radar experimental vessel. After the war the ISLE OF SARK resumed her station, being finally sold in 1960 and broken up in the yard of Van Heygen Freres at Ghent in Belgium a year later. Among her commanders were Captains Large, F. Cantle, Hatchley and H. Breuilly.

BRITTANY

BRITTANY

The second vessel of this name on the Channel Islands mail service the BRITTANY was built in 1933 by Denny Brothers of Dumbarton. A twin screw turbine steamer of 1,522 tons gross, 294 feet in length with a 39 foot beam, her engines developing 2,500 h.p. with a speed of 16 knots. She could carry 850 passengers. BRITTANY was originally built for the Southern Railway Company's Jersey to France service, but she also served on the Alderney, Sark and Cherbourg routes. During the war BRITTANY was at first used as a transport at Dunkirk, later she was at Colombo as an anti-submarine net layer and saw service at West Africa, Seychelles, Panama, Bombay and later assisted with the invasion of Southern France. After the war she resumed her Jersey to St. Malo route until she was finally withdrawn in 1962, sold to Finland in 1963 and was re-named ALANDSFARJAN. Among her commanders were Captains Withers, Trout, Campbell, Caws, Breuilly and Picot.

ST. DAVID and ST. PATRICK (sister ships)

These ships were the second of these names the first ST. DAVID being lost during the war at Anzio, and the first ST. PATRICK was bombed in the Irish sea.

The ST. DAVID and ST. PATRICK were sister ships built by Cammel Laird & Company of Birkenhead in 1947–8, the ST. DAVID being 3,352 tons and the ST. PATRICK 3,482 tons, they were each 321 feet in length and 48 feet in breadth, twin screw steam turbine engines. The ST. DAVID could carry 1,300 passengers and 50 cars. Their normal route was Fish-

91

guard to Rosslare, but from the 4th February, 1948, the ST. PATRICK had been used regularly as a relief vessel to the Channel Islands, and in 1963 she was transferred to the Southampton to St. Malo route to replace the FALAISE, after being purchased by British Railways in 1959.

The ST. DAVID first came to the Channel Islands late in 1947, but never came as often as her sister ship. She was sold to a Greek company in 1971.

ST. PATRICK

FALAISE

The FALAISE built by William Denny at Dumbarton in 1947 was a twin screw turbine steamer of 3,710 tons, 311 feet in length with a 48 foot beam, she had a speed of 20½ knots, and was fitted with radio telephone, Radar and Denny-Brown stabilizers. FALAISE was acquired by the British Transport Commission from Southern Railways in 1948. Her first trip to Jersey was on the 19th July, 1947, but the FALAISE could only be described as a relief vessel as far as the Channel Islands were concerned because apart from taking

FALAISE

cruises, her normal route was Southampton to St. Malo. In 1964 FALAISE was converted to a car ferry and was then able to carry 750 passengers and 100 cars.

NORMANNIA (2)
The NORMANNIA (the second vessel of this name) was built by William Denny of Dumbarton in 1952, a twin screw turbine steamer of 3,543 gross tons, 309 feet in length with a 48 foot beam, her 8,000 h.p. engines give her a speed of 19½ knots, she carried 1,400 passengers. NORMANNIA was a frequent visitor to these islands. Her normal route was Southampton to Le Havre. In 1964 the NORMANNIA was converted to a car ferry on the Dover to Boulogne to Calais route.

CAESAREA and SARNIA (sister ships)
Finally we come to the last and most impressive of all the mail ships to come to the islands, the splendid CAESAREA and SARNIA named after the alleged Roman names of Jersey and Guernsey. Built in 1960 by J. Samuel White & Company Ltd. at Cowes in the Isle of Wight, they are twin screw turbine steamers, of 4,174 gross tons, 322 feet in length and a 51 foot beam, they have two pamatrada steam turbines, two three-bladed 10 foot diameter propellers giving a speed of 20 knots, they have a raked stem, rounded stern, two tripod masts, single funnels, fitted with Denny-Brown stabilizers and a stern and bow

rudder, five decks, 25 double and 12 single cabins, 44 sleeping berths, 6 fibre-glass life-boats and 45 inflatable rafts. They both can take 1,400 passengers and have a crew of 78, these vessels cost £1,500,000 each.

CAESAREA first came to Jersey (showing the flag) on the 18th November, 1960, and the SARNIA on the 17th June, 1961.

In 1971, 146 new aircraft style seats were fitted in each of these vessels to replace wooden or table chairs on decks and in the cafeteria. The improvement taking place during the annual overhaul.

NORMANNIA   JERSEY EVENING POST

LAUNCHING OF THE 'CAESAREA' AT COWES   JERSEY EVENING POST

ARRIVAL OF THE 'CAESAREA' AT JERSEY   JERSEY EVENING POST

SARNIA   BRITISH RAIL

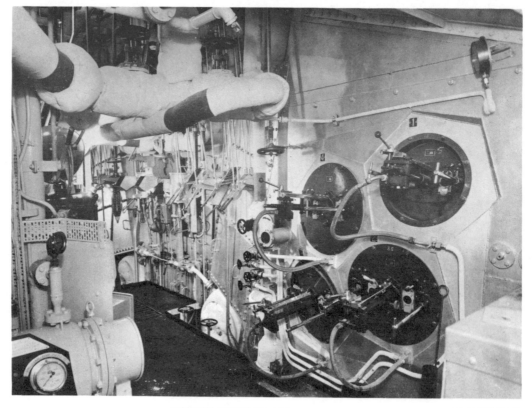

BOILER ROOM OF THE SARNIA   BRITISH RAIL

RESTAURANT OF THE SARNIA

GALLEY OF THE SARNIA

Conclusion

In May, 1961, Southampton was closed as a Channel Island passenger port and all mail-ships were re-routed to Weymouth, this being done as an economy measure by the British Transport Commission. This was a sad day indeed, for Southampton had been the most favoured port of Channel Islands traffic for several hundred years.

Thus we come to the end of this short history having observed the improvements in size, speed, power and comfort of these ships, and it is indeed a far cry from the EARL OF CHESTERFIELD packet of 80 tons in 1794 to the CAESAREA of 4,174 tons of 1960.

HOVERCRAFT VT1–001   JERSEY EVENING POST

It is a fitting finale to this book and somewhat of a coincidence as these words are being written, that Britains second largest hovercraft, the V.T.–1 has arrived in Jersey to begin a month of government trials between this island and France.

Able to carry 146 passengers with ten cars, the V.T.–1 has a top speed of 40 knots she has two Avco lycoming T.F. 2030 gas turbine engines, each rated at 1,850 h.p. two controllable pitch propellers and eight 8 foot diameter fans to provide air for the cushion.

It is significant to note that the V.T.–1 arrived in Jersey only four hours after leaving Gosport, a distance of 124 miles.

Bibliography...

A History of the Great Western Railway ... ... G.A. Sekon

A History of the Southern Railway ... ... Dendy Marshall

Chronique De Jersey ... ... (Newspapers)

Cross Channel & Coastal Paddle Steamers ... ... Burtt

English Channel Packet Boats ... ... Grassman & McLean

Gazette de l'Isle ... ... (Newspapers)

Jersey Evening Post ... ... (Newspapers)

Jersey Argus ... ... (Newspapers)

Jersey Chamber of Commerce Records

Jersey Times & British Press ... ... (Newspapers)

Life of John Bazin ... ... James Crabb (1837)

Morning News ... ... Jersey (Newspapers)

Paper on Channel Islands Postal History by J.M.Y. Trotter ... Societe Guernesiaise

Paper on Early C.I. Steamers J.M. David ... ... Societe Guernesiaise

Publications of the C.I. Specialists Society ... ... (Postal History)

Scrapbooks at the Museum of the Societe Jersiaise

Steamers of British Railways ... ... Clegg & Styring

The Great Western at Weymouth ... ... J.H. Lucking (David and Charles)

The Star (Guernsey) ... ... (Newspapers)

A Chronological Table of

Vessels in the C.I. Mail Service 1794–1971

NAME	BUILT	RIG	REMARKS
ROYAL CHARLOTTE	Pre–1794	Cutter	1st P.O. Packet. Ended Service 1795
EARL OF CHESTERFIELD	Pre–1794	cutter	sold in 1806
ROVER	Pre–1794	cutter	2nd official P.O. packet
CHESTERFIELD (1)	?	cutter	captured by French 1811
CHESTERFIELD (2)	?	cutter	False packet ceased 1814
GENERAL DOYLE	1803	cutter	sold 1809
FRANCIS FREELING	1811	cutter	wrecked in 1826
RAPID	?	cutter	armed scout, relief only
MARY	?	cutter	armed scout, relief only
BRITANNIA	?	cutter	armed scout, relief only
BRILLIANT	?	cutter	armed scout, relief only
SIR SYDNEY SMITH	?	cutter	armed scout, relief only
SIR WILLIAM CURTIS	?	cutter	armed scout, relief only
HINCHINBROOK	1811	cutter	wrecked in 1826
COUNTESS OF LIVERPOOL	1813	cutter	sold to the post office 1827
WATERSPRITE (later H.M.S. WILDFIRE)	1826	wooden paddle steamer	broken up in 1888
IVANHOE	1820	wooden paddle steamer	withdrawn 1837
METEOR	1821	wooden paddle steamer	wrecked in 1830
FLAMER (later H.M.S. FEARLESS)	1831	wooden paddle steamer	withdrawn in 1845
H.M.S. PLUTO	1831	wooden paddle steamer	replaced FLAMER 6 months
H.M.S. DASHER	1837	wooden paddle steamer	withdrawn 1845
H.M.S. CUCKOO	1822	wooden paddle steamer	withdrawn 1845
SOUTH WESTERN	1843	iron paddle steamer	sold in 1863
TRANSIT	1835	wooden paddle steamer	ended as a coal hulk 1860
WONDER	1844	iron paddle steamer	sold for scrap 1875
CALPE	1835	wooden paddle steamer	mail short time only
LADY DE SAUMAREZ	1835	wooden paddle steamer	broken up in 1853
ATALANTA	1836	wooden paddle steamer	ended as a coal hulk 1869

NAME	BUILT	RIG	REMARKS
MONARCH	1836	wooden paddle steamer	converted to a barque 1849
COURIER	1847	iron paddle steamer	broken up c.1874
DISPATCH	1847	iron paddle steamer	withdrawn in 1888
EXPRESS	1847	iron paddle steamer	wrecked in 1859
ALLIANCE	1855	iron paddle steamer	broken up in 1900
AQUILA	1854	iron paddle steamer	sold in 1889
CYGNUS	1854	iron paddle steamer	sold in 1889
BRIGHTON	1856	iron paddle steamer	wrecked in 1887
GREAT WESTERN	1867	iron paddle steamer	6 months only (sold 1891)
SOUTHAMPTON	1860	iron paddle steamer	broken up in 1898
NORMANDY	1863	iron paddle steamer	wrecked in 1870
BRITTANY	1864	iron paddle steamer	broken up in 1900
GRIFFIN	1858	iron screw steamer	sold in 1895
ST. MALO	1865	iron screw steamer	broken up in 1906
CAESAREA (1)	1867	iron screw steamer	wrecked in 1884
WAVERLEY	1865	iron paddle steamer	wrecked in 1873
HAVRE	1856	iron paddle steamer	wrecked in 1875
ALICE	1859	iron paddle steamer	a hulk in 1888
FANNIE	1859	iron paddle steamer	sold c.1887
HONFLEUR	1873	iron screw steamer	sold in 1900
GUERNSEY	1874	iron screw steamer	wrecked in 1915
SOUTH WESTERN (2)	1874	iron screw steamer	torpedoed in 1918
DIANA	1876	iron screw steamer	wrecked in 1895
CALEDONIA	1876	iron screw steamer	wrecked in 1881
ELLA	1881	iron screw steamer	sold in 1913
HILDA	1882	iron screw steamer	wrecked in 1905
LAURA	1885	steel screw steamer	sold and later wrecked in the Bahamas
GAEL	1867	iron paddle steamer	sold in 1891
LYNX	1888	twin screw steamer	converted 1912 broken up 1925
ANTELOPE	1889	twin screw steamer	sold in 1913
GAZELLE	1889	twin screw steamer	converted 1908, sold 1925
DORA	1889	single screw steamer	sold in 1901
FREDERICA	1890	steel twin screw steamer	sold in 1911
LYDIA	1890	steel twin screw steamer	sold in 1919
STELLA	1890	steel twin screw steamer	wrecked in 1899
IBEX	1890	steel twin screw steamer	broken up in 1926—7
COLUMBIA	1894	twin screw steamer	sold in 1912
ALMA	1894	twin screw steamer	sold in 1912
VICTORIA	1896	screw steamer	sold in 1919
ROEBUCK	1897	twin screw steamer	sank in 1915 whilst R.N.
REINDEER	1897	twin screw	taken off service in 1925
VERA	1898	twin screw	broken up in 1933

NAME	BUILT	RIG	REMARKS
ALBERTA	1900	twin screw	out of service 1929, sold 1930
GREAT WESTERN (3)	1902	twin screw	sold in 1933
GREAT SOUTHERN	1902	twin screw	sold in 1934
PRINCESS ENA	1906	twin screw turbine	caught fire and sank 1935
CAESAREA (2)	1910	triple screw turbine	sold in 1923
SARNIA	1910	triple screw turbine	torpedoed in 1918
NORMANNIA	1910	twin screw turbine	lost at Dunkirk 1940
HANTONIA	1911	twin screw turbine	broken up in 1952
LORINA	1918	twin screw turbine	lost at Dunkirk 1940
ARDENA	1915	single screw steamer	sold in 1934
DINARD	1924	twin screw turbine	withdrawn 1958, sold 1959
ST. BRIAC	1924	twin screw turbine	lost in 1942
ST. HELIER	1925	twin screw turbine	broken up in 1961
ST. JULIEN	1925	twin screw turbine	broken up in 1961
ST. PATRICK	1930	twin screw turbine	bombed and lost in 1941
ISLE OF JERSEY	1930	twin screw turbine	sold in 1960
ISLE OF GUERNSEY	1930	twin screw turbine	broken up in 1961
ISLE OF SARK	1932	twin screw turbine	broken up in 1961
BRITTANY (2)	1933	twin screw turbine	sold to Finland 1963
ST. DAVID	1947	twin screw (oil)	came as relief only Sold to a Greek Co. in 1971
ST. PATRICK (2)	1947	twin screw (oil)	transferred to Soton to St. Malo
FALAISE	1947	twin screw (oil)	converted to car ferry 1964
NORMANNIA (2)	1952	twin screw (oil)	converted to car ferry 1964
CAESAREA (3)	1960	twin screw (oil)	322 feet in length
SARNIA (2)	1960	twin screw (oil)	cost £1,500,000

Even up to the present day numerous cargo vessels have been used to carry the Channel Islands mail under various circumstances, i.e. Wartime, peak periods and relief. They have not been included in this table.

Index of All Vessels Named in this Book

PAGE (TEXT) *(Illus.)*   PAGE